Introduction

Weddings are supposed to be the happiest of occasions but sometimes things go terribly wrong and tragedies occur. Brides and grooms commit suicide, accidents, illness and death intervene and the petty jealousies and concerns that dog people's lives can often get blown out of proportion, with terrifying consequences.

What follows is a collection of wedding disasters, some macabre, some frankly bizarre, but all equally harrowing for those concerned.

I have tried to piece the various stories together from contemporary newspaper reports but, much as today, not everything that is reported in the press is entirely accurate and there were frequent discrepancies between different publications. Where there is a direct conflict of information between sources, I have included an explanatory footnote but otherwise I have stuck with the most commonly quoted variant. I have also used the Counties that were applicable at the time of each particular incident – so, for example, while Peterborough is now in Cambridgeshire, it was historically in Northamptonshire.

Every effort has been made to clear copyright; however, my apologies to anyone I might have inadvertently missed. I can assure you that it was not deliberate but an oversight on my part.

I have several people to thank for their assistance in compiling this book. Preston Digital Archives and Peter Barton both granted their permission to use photographs as illustrations, while Lynda Bolding took the magnificent photograph for the book's cover. My husband Richard has done an amazing job as my proof reader and as supplier of cups of tea while I was writing and, as always, I am extremely grateful for his help and support.

So, let the mayhem commence…

South West

Newton, Dorset

Woodman Percy Thomas Brownsea and Beatrice Sheen had known each other for more than five years when she broke off their engagement in favour of another man.

Throughout his time in the armed forces, Beatrice had written to Brownsea, her letters beginning '*My own dearest, darling, devoted and loving husband-to-be...*'. The content of the correspondence showed that the couple had not only enjoyed a passionate sexual intimacy, but that Beatrice was only too keen for it to resume when Brownsea returned.

Beatrice had a child by another man while Brownsea was away serving his country but he forgave her and bought her a ring when he was demobbed. However, In October 1946, Beatrice dumped him in favour of her cousin, Uriah 'Hughie' Jones. Whereas Brownsea had very little income and very few prospects, Jones had a successful business as a sand and gravel merchant and was therefore in a much better position to marry than Beatrice's former fiancé.

Brownsea was devastated and continuously begged Beatrice to reconsider. He refused to take back the engagement ring he had bought for her, so she eventually sold it and gave him the money.

Beatrice and Hughie's wedding was planned for 1st January 1947 and on 28th December, the couple went to the pub with Beatrice's brother, William. They were joined by Brownsea and by all accounts, the foursome enjoyed drinks and games of darts together until the pub closed, when Beatrice and Hughie went off alone.

As they later sat on a sofa kissing at Hughie's home, his head suddenly fell onto her shoulder. 'Oh, dear, Beat' he groaned, before rolling off the sofa onto the floor. Those were the last words that he spoke.

The couple had been shot, with Hughie taking sixty-six shotgun pellets in his head and Beatrice nine in the left-hand side of her face.

When Brownsea was later asked to account for his movements that evening, he admitted firing a gun through the window of the bungalow, saying that he had intended to frighten Beatrice. Told that Hughie had been fatally wounded, Brownsea promptly fainted.

Brownsea was charged with wilful murder and appeared at the Winchester Assizes on 20th March 1947. He pleaded 'not guilty', claiming to have drunk seven or eight pints of beer and some gin on the night in question and stating that he had not noticed anybody in the room before firing his borrowed gun through the window.

The prosecution maintained that the shooting had been done in '...a blaze of jealousy and malice'. Brownsea claimed that he no longer wished to marry Beatrice and denied asking her repeatedly to take him back, insisting that he had only asked once or twice before realising that he was no longer interested in becoming her husband.

When Brownsea's home was searched, a package of Beatrice's letters to him was found with a covering letter addressed to Hughie that read: *'Dear Sir, just a few lines wishing you the best of luck in your forthcoming marriage to Miss Beatrice Sheen. I was engaged to be married to her. When she found out you had a lorry, money and a house, I was cast aside. Here are some of the letters from your future wife.'*

Beatrice was in court to give evidence against her former fiancé. 'What business was it of his whether I was getting married or not?' she asked the defence counsel. 'I had finished with him.'

The prosecution argued that the killing was '... a deliberate shooting motivated by the blind jealousy of a man who had been thrown over after a long and passionate love affair'. Beatrice's letters to Brownsea were described as '... having a degree of passion and coarseness and the utmost intimacy, designed to excite him in every possible way.' The shot that killed Jones was fired from directly outside the window of the bungalow and the prosecution asserted that Brownsea could not have failed to see the couple kissing on the sofa inside.

The defence stressed the fact that Brownsea, Beatrice and Hughie had been socialising in the pub earlier that evening and relations between them had been friendly.

Nobody argued about whether or not Brownsea had fired the gun – it was agreed that he had. The prosecution believed it had been fired with intent, making Brownsea guilty of murder, while the defence insisted that there had been no malice intended but, under the influence of alcohol, Brownsea had done something terribly foolish, which had the most tragic consequence. The jury took the side of the defence, finding Brownsea guilty of the lesser charge of manslaughter. He was sentenced to seven years' imprisonment.

Chagford, Devon

On 11th October 1641, Mary Whiddon (or Whyddon) from Chagford looked radiant as she walked up the aisle of Chagford Church to meet her groom. With the ceremony preformed, the newlyweds walked out of the church as man and wife but as they reached the steps, there was a loud bang and Mary fell to the floor, a red stain spreading across the bodice of her white silk gown.

Mary had been courting another man, who she jilted in favour of her husband. Her spurned lover was unbearably jealous and, as the date of the wedding drew nearer, his anger reached fever pitch and he would viciously malign her to anyone who could be persuaded to listen.

Now as Mary lay bleeding on the church steps, her devastated husband sank to his knees and cradled her in his arms but she died where she had fallen, shot by the jealous lover whose affections she had rejected.

Mary's body was buried beneath the chancel of the church, her last resting place marked by a stone slab set into the floor. Her epitaph reads:

'Mary Whiddon, daughter of Oliver Whiddon, who died in 1641.

Reader, would'st though know who here is laid,

Behold a matron, yet a maid.

A Mary for the better part

But dry thine eyes, why wilt thou weep

Such damselles do not die, but sleep.'

Mary's ghost, dressed in a period wedding dress, is said to wander within the churchyard and also at her home, Whiddon Park, especially around the time of her wedding anniversary.

In 1971, another daughter of the house was to be married at the same church and awoke on the morning of her wedding to find the apparition of a sad-looking woman in a wedding dress standing in the doorway of her bedroom. On that occasion, the bride placed her bouquet on Mary's grave as a mark of respect, a tradition that has since been continued by other brides.

It is said that the legend of Mary Whiddon was the inspiration for part of R.B. Blackmore's book *Lorna Doone*. Blackmore is known to have spent time in the Chagford area and it is almost certain that he was familiar with the story and that it inspired him to create a similar storyline.

Winchcombe, Gloucestershire

Thirty-nine-year-old butcher Frederick Fawdry of Gloucester Street, Winchcombe, married Miss Elizabeth Matthew on 15 May 1917, the couple having been courting for almost thirteen years. It wasn't the first time that a wedding had been arranged between the couple but Fawdry kept getting cold feet. Eventually, on 28th April 1917, Elizabeth wrote to her fiancé, giving him an ultimatum

'Dear Fred, I am writing to tell you how wretched I have been since Thursday. You must settle this at once. You said once or twice that we should marry. If you want me, Fred, I will forgive and forget all that is past and devote my life to your welfare and happiness. But it must be done at once. We can go to a registry office here on Monday and I would come home on Tuesday. I have humbled myself to you because I still love you; but you must do one thing or another because I have to go back to Winchcombe to make arrangements. If you still wish that we should part you must give me the amount of money I asked you before Wednesday. I want you to consider for your own good and respecting what I have written, to act on your own principle of not saying anything to anyone, as it only concerns you and I. Write to me tomorrow and tell me what you intend doing and I will meet you anywhere in Gloucester. Married or parted, I shall always have happy thoughts of the past but of the future, I shall not dare think. If we part, you must keep away from me forever.'

Frederick was known as a quiet, rather inoffensive man, with a history of suffering from anxiety and bad nerves. In March 1917, he consulted his doctor, Dr Cox, telling him that his nerves were 'gone' and that he felt quite overwhelmed, as if he were going to fall down. On 6th April, Cox saw Fawdry again, this time in the presence of a Relieving Officer and magistrate Mr Adlard. Apparently Fawdry's friends had been looking after him but now claimed that his mind had completely given way and they were unable to cope. Cox promptly certified him as a person of unsound mind, authorising his admission to an asylum for treatment.

Mr Adlard had a better idea. He managed to find someone who was willing to take Fawdry away to the seaside for some rest and recuperation and accordingly Fawdry was despatched to Torquay and Weston-Super-Mare, where he might convalesce and recover. He returned after just three days, at which time he seemed very depressed. Cox saw him ten days later, noting that he now seemed somewhat manic, although he did not believe him to be either suicidal or homicidal.

When Fawdry received his fiancée's letter, it seemed to spur him into action and a wedding was quickly arranged. Despite Fawdry arriving at the church more than thirty minutes late and still wearing his butcher's smock, the ceremony went ahead and the couple returned to Fawdry's shop, where according to his housekeeper Miss Rose Page, they spent a very happy day together.

Gloucester Street, Winchcombe (author's collection)

After Fawdry had been to the pub alone for a quick drink, the newlyweds retired to bed at ten o'clock and the following morning, Fawdry rose at five o'clock in order to slaughter a bullock, returning afterwards to have breakfast with his wife. Rose noticed that he seemed very quiet and morose but this was not unusual and she thought no more of it.

At just after eight o'clock, Rose heard a terrible scream, then a thud coming from the kitchen, where the Fawdrys were breakfasting.

She rushed to investigate, finding Elizabeth lying on the floor in a pool of blood and Fred hacking at his own throat with a knife.

Rose screamed and neighbour George Cutting ran into the house to see what was happening. Cutting quickly sent for a doctor and the police but by the time they arrived, both Mr and Mrs Fawdry were beyond any assistance. Three letters were found in Fred's pocket – a letter from Elizabeth dated January 17th 1917 and signed '...fondest love and kisses', his fiancée's ultimatum letter and a letter written in his own hand, which had not been posted. This letter, dated 29th April, read: *'Dear Lizzie, If I am well enough, I am going to Gloucester tomorrow and shall come and see you. I was weak and low yesterday and today, as a time like I have had takes a bit of getting over. I shall see you at the market. Hope you are keeping in good health. I am yours etc Fred. Excuse pencil.'*

An inquest was held at Winchcombe Town Hall by coroner John Waghorne, where the jury found a verdict of wilful murder against Frederick Fawdry, who then committed suicide.

Coombe Keynes, Dorset

Twenty-four-year-old Kenneth Arthur Brimley had seen active service in the World War before returning home to St Neots, Cambridgeshire, to work with his father as a carpenter. He had been badly wounded by shrapnel at the Battle of the Somme, since when he had suffered from headaches and had been 'rather excitable' in temperament. However, his biggest concern was that, after his injury, he began to go bald and was now left with just a small amount of hair on the back of his head.

Brimley had been engaged to a girl from Leeds for two years and, as the date of their wedding approached, he became ever more agitated about his baldness.

On 28th May 1923, he left home to travel to Leeds for his wedding in two days' time. He took with him a case containing his newly purchased wedding suit. On the day before the wedding, he sent two letters to relatives, one saying that he was in Nottingham and was going to have a look round and the other saying he was heading to Scotland. That same day, his suitcase arrived back from King's Cross Station, the address label written in his own handwriting.

Brimley's body was found on his wedding day. He was nowhere near Nottingham, Scotland or Leeds but was instead lying face down in a pond on a farm at Coombe Keynes, near the Tank Corps Centre where he had undertaken his military training. He left no note but had obviously gone into the pond intentionally as his raincoat was left neatly folded on the bank.

Coroner Mr C.H. Watts–Parkinson held an inquest on his death, at which the only reason that anyone could suggest for Brimley's actions were his concerns about his baldness. He had no financial worries, was on the best of terms with his fiancée and was said to be very much looking forward to getting married. The jury found a verdict of 'drowned while of unsound mind.'

Taunton, Somerset

In 1746, Mary Hamilton appeared at the Somerset Quarter Sessions. Mary's crime – for which the court could not agree on a name – was that she had masqueraded as a man named either George or Charles Hamilton and had married no less than fourteen women.

Her most recent wife was a lady named Mary Price, who married her 'husband' at St Cuthbert's Church in Wells and had lived with and bedded 'him' for three months. Mary Price told the court that she had never suspected that her husband was in fact a woman, due mainly to the '...vile and deceitful practices, not fit to be mentioned' that occurred in the privacy of their marital bedroom.

While the court could not agree on the nature of Mary Hamilton's offence, nor give a name for it, they did agree that she was 'an uncommon notorious cheat' and should therefore be publicly flogged in the towns of Taunton, Glastonbury, Wells and Shepton Mallet, before serving a six-month prison sentence.

Countess Wear, Exeter, Devon

Having been engaged for a year, thirty-two-year-old cook Thomas Clarke was due to marry Lilian Bowden on 6th January 1932. All the arrangements were made for the wedding and reception and a house had been furnished, ready for the couple to live in after their honeymoon.

On 3rd January, Thomas visited Lilian at her home and showed her £10 that he had saved up, telling her that he was going to buy the wedding ring the next day. That same evening, Thomas asked his brother Samuel if he would be best man but Samuel told him that he couldn't, as he would be unable to get time off work. 'It's all right, I'll get someone else', Thomas reassured him.

Thomas then went out and was not seen again until the morning of his wedding, when he was found dead on the railway line at Countess Wear. Although one of his legs had been severed, the cause of death was a fracture of the skull, which doctors said could have resulted from being hit by a train.

At the inquest on his death, everyone was in complete agreement that Thomas was looking forward to his wedding and that he and his bride-to-be were very much in love. He lived in Torquay and worked at the Imperial Hotel there, so nobody could quite understand how he came to be found on a railway line near Exeter. The most mysterious thing was that only 1d was found in his jacket pocket and his fiancée could not comprehend how he could possibly have spent almost £10 in so short a time.

The Imperial Hotel, Torquay (author's collection)

It was speculated that Thomas might have been going to see another of his brothers, who lived in Exeter, to ask him if he would be best man but that didn't explain the missing money. In addition, Thomas's family told the inquest that, whenever he visited his brother, he always travelled by bus.

Railway employees testified that there had been no reports of train doors being found open, although the deceased's cap had been found under a bridge, where the ballast between the lines was disturbed as though someone had jumped or fallen from the road onto the lines. Twenty-eight trains had passed along that particular length of track between the last sighting of Thomas alive and the finding of his body. Each train had been carefully examined and none showed any trace of any impact.

The coroner told the inquest jury that there was no evidence to show how Clarke came to be on the line, or indeed, why he was even in the area at all. It was impossible to know whether he was suffering from any illness, loss of memory or whether he had any worries, financial or otherwise. There were many possibilities connected with the tragedy and numerous things that could have happened. Clarke could have fallen out of a train window, although in that case, he might have been expected to have a train ticket on his person. He might have deliberately placed himself on the line but none of his family could think of any reason why he might have done so. He might have been walking along the line and fallen down but there was not enough evidence to tell. The coroner therefore instructed the jury that the only possible verdict was an open one and accordingly a verdict of 'found dead' was returned, the jury, being unable to decide on precisely how or even why Clarke had perished.

Mr Justice Denman (author's collection)

Bristol, Gloucestershire

On 15th November 1875, fifty-four-year-old Thomas Buller went for a drink after work at The Foresters Arms pub in Bristol. He was accompanied by his workmates John 'Jack' Richards and Henry Click.

While they were drinking, a man named Edward Clapp came into the pub. Nineteen-year-old Clapp had been married to Ann Smith only that morning and the couple were celebrating.

When the three workmates left the pub, another man was just walking in and there was a bit of larking about, during which Mrs Clapp was accidentally jostled by John Richards. As they walked outside, Clapp grabbed Richards and asked him 'What did you insult my wife like that for?'

'Ted, he didn't insult me. He did not touch me' protested his wife but there was no pacifying Clapp, who promptly slapped Richards on both cheeks. Richards and Clapp began scuffling and Richards either fell or was knocked over.

Thomas Buller reached to pull him up, saying 'Come on, Jack, don't have any more bother' Scarcely had the words left his mouth when Clapp punched him in the face and knocked him over, the back of his head striking the kerb.

His friends tried to give him brandy to revive him and, when that didn't work, they took him to hospital. Sadly, Buller never regained consciousness and died soon afterwards. The cause of his death was later determined to be 'concussion of the brain.'

Coroner Mr H.S. Wasborough held an inquest, at which the jury returned a verdict of manslaughter against Clapp, who was sent for trial at the next Bristol Assizes. Before Mr Justice Denman, Clapp pleaded guilty to manslaughter but the prosecution had been instructed not to press the case. Denman remarked that he hoped that this was not the way in which wedding days were usually spent in

Bristol, before binding Clapp over and discharging him, warning him to be kind and gentle to everyone in future.

Isle Abbotts, Somerset

On 18th August 1907, clerk Arthur John Burt and his best man were waiting at the village church in Isle Abbotts, Somerset, for the arrival of the bride, Miss Emily Eliza Hooper, when suddenly the vicar began the service. Burt pointed out the fact that the bride had not yet put in an appearance, at which Reverend James H.C. Taylor rather petulantly stopped talking to await her arrival.

When Emily got to church, Taylor began again but within a few words, it became obvious that he was performing the burial service rather than a wedding. 'I commit these people to the ground, earth to earth…' he intoned, as the groom and members of the congregation tried in vain to stop him.

By then, Emily was weeping and was on the verge of fainting. Burt remonstrated again with the vicar, who segued into the baptismal service before lapsing into an incoherent babble.

Once the wedding was finally completed, Burt had his doubts about the legality of the ceremony and demanded that another clergyman should be summoned to sort out the mess. The best man set off for Ilminster on his bicycle, while another female guest cycled off in the opposite direction towards Ilton. Meanwhile, Taylor tried to leave the church and, when the groom tried to prevent him from doing so, he ripped off his surplice and threw it onto a tombstone in the churchyard.

In due course, another vicar arrived and the wedding ceremony was performed properly. However, the whole ceremony took two and a half hours, meaning that by the time it was finally solemnised it was after the legal hour.

The newlywed couple received a letter of apology from the Bishop of Bath and Wells for the '...extremely painful circumstances they were placed in on account of the disgraceful conduct and condition of Mr Taylor'. The Bishop told them that Taylor had been suspended from his duties pending a full investigation.

When the contemporary press tried to talk to Taylor, he declared that his legal representative had told him to make no comment. 'I felt ill, that's all' he said and then, ignoring his legal advisor, he went on to blame sunstroke, the death of his daughter, bankruptcy through building the vicarage, insomnia, mental depression and an internal complaint for the debacle.

Torrington, Devon

Twenty-six-year-old Valentine Annie Fisher Copp was set to marry her sweetheart Thomas Wooland on 13th February 1922 but as the date grew closer, Valentine got cold feet and told Thomas the wedding was off.

At the time, she was living with her married sister, Hilda Mary Cudmore at Peters Marsland and, when Hilda asked her sister what had happened, all Valentine would say on the subject was that she was never going to get married.

She moped around the house for almost a month before Thomas came to see her and the couple had a long chat. By the time Thomas left, the wedding was back on again, the date set for 18th March, and Valentine seemed much brighter and happier than she had of late.

Two days before the wedding, she was heard tossing and turning in her bed all night and, when she got up the next morning, she announced to her sister 'I can't get married. It's no use.' She seemed to fall into a deep depression and threatened to drown herself or take poison, before leaving the house, saying that she was going for a walk.

Her concerned sister started to follow her but Valentine rounded on her and told her that she wanted to be alone. Hilda had two young children at home, besides which she was not yet dressed, so she reluctantly let her sister walk away.

Valentine went to their aunt's house, where she spoke to her aunt, uncle and cousin before setting off again. It was to be the last time she was seen alive, as her body was pulled from the River Torridge later that day.

Coroner George W.F. Brown held an inquest on her death at Torrington Cottage Hospital and Thomas Wooland stated that Valentine had been hot and cold about the idea of getting married. 'Sometimes she wanted to, sometimes she didn't', he explained. Then, having heard from Hilda Cudmore, the coroner adjourned the inquest so that Hilda's husband, William, and their aunt, uncle and cousin could be called to say why, knowing her state of mind, they had not restrained Valentine and prevented her from going to her death.

Despite admitting that he had told her to 'Cheer up, have some tea and go back to bed' on the morning of her death, William Cudmore claimed that he hadn't realised that his sister-in-law was depressed and had not heard her threaten to kill herself. He had spoken to her at length about her fiancé, telling her that not one man in a dozen would have come back to her again, as Wooland had, after she called off their wedding. He admitted to the coroner that he realised that there was something bothering Valentine but said that he had done all he could to help her.

Valentine's uncle, Henry Hooper, said that Valentine was a little pale and seemed depressed when she visited and he too had told her to 'Cheer up'. He told the coroner that he didn't believe that there was much wrong with her or that she needed to be watched. His son, Lewis, said that his cousin had simply said that she was going for a nice walk. When Hilda had visited them later that day, Henry and Lewis both insisted that she had said nothing to them about her concerns for Valentine's wellbeing, even though by that time, she had reported her sister missing to the police.

The coroner obviously didn't believe Henry and Lewis, saying that it was not a woman's way to keep such things to herself. When the inquest jury returned a verdict that Valentine had drowned herself while of unsound mind, the coroner closed the proceedings by remarking that, had Valentine been prevented from going out, she would still have been alive.

Thorncombe, Dorset

William Bragg had farmed Broadridge Farm in Thorncombe all his life and, when he retired, his two sons took over the running of the farm in partnership, with William living in one half of the house and the two brothers in the other. They shared a housekeeper, Mary Elizabeth Probert, and before long, she and the eldest brother fell in love.

When Leonard John 'Corrie' Bragg and Mary wanted to get married, it was decided to split the partnership between the two brothers and Corrie and Mary agreed to buy a farm in Wendover, Buckinghamshire. However, his younger brother, Harold William Bragg, was unable to find a suitable farm and so their father agreed to let him stay on at Broadridge until one was found.

This decision upset Corrie, who would ideally have liked to stay on at Broadridge without his brother. He hated the idea of moving to Buckinghamshire, telling people 'I don't want to leave the old place. I have lived here all my life and I want to settle here for the rest of my life.'

The ill-feeling between the two brothers mounted. Harold was jealous of his brother's relationship with their housekeeper and Corrie was upset because his brother was to stay at home, while he had to move away.

Matters came to a head on 20th February 1935, just a few days before Corrie and Mary were due to marry. Their farm labourer noticed that the brothers were not out at work as usual when he arrived that morning, and, getting no response to his knocks on the farmhouse door, he roused William Bragg, who fetched a ladder and put it up to a bedroom window. To his horror, he found both of his sons dead, Harold lying on the bed and Corrie on the floor, with a shotgun between them.

The coroner held two inquests, reading out a letter that Corrie had left for his fiancée, which read: *'Oh, Mary dear. I am terribly sorry I am passing into the next world. Knowing my experience here will make me pine away at Wendover, I think it is best to have it over now'.* The letter continued to discuss some money that Corrie had sent his fiancée, then concluded *'My head is terribly bad'*.

The inquest concluded that Corrie had shot his brother then committed suicide while of unsound mind.

Note: The farm is sometimes reported to be at Chard Junction in Somerset. (It lies very near the border of both counties)

Stoneybridge, Par, Cornwall

On 15th January 1930, Walter Longston spotted a van that had crashed into some railings at Stoneybridge, Par. When Longston went for a closer look, he found a man lying underneath the van between the front and the back wheels. Obviously very badly injured, the man was still conscious, although unable to explain how the accident happened.

Dr Noel Blaney was called and determined that the van driver, William Thomas Reed, had a fractured spine and apparent internal injuries and bleeding. Reed was sent to Falmouth Hospital, where he died soon after admission.

At an inquest held by Coroner Mr. E.L. Carlyon, it was stated that Reed was employed by the Falmouth District Steam Laundry Co. Ltd. as a driver. His boss, Mr Pearce-Rogers told the inquest that he suspected that Reed had tried to start the van while it was in gear and had been thrown out. 'He was due to be married the next day and was no doubt in a hurry to get home' theorised Pearce-Rogers.

The inquest found that Reed had died as a consequence of injuries sustained in a road accident, although there was nothing to suggest how the accident occurred.

Tavistock, Devon

After their wedding at two o'clock on 22nd January 1919, twenty-one-year-old Winnie Sims (formerly Metters) and her husband William John Sims celebrated with their families at The Golden Lion Inn at Tavistock. The proprietor, Mr J. Vigars, had kindly allowed the wedding party the use of his car and chauffeur for the day and after taking the bridegroom's parents to the station to catch their train back to Plymouth, some of the younger guests at the wedding decided to take advantage of the landlord's generosity and go for a jaunt to nearby Mary Tavy.

Driven by chauffeur Percy John Gregory, the bride and groom and two of the bride's cousins – Joseph and Nellie Craze – reached Mary Tavy and stopped at The Royal Standard Inn, where Gregory, Joseph Craze and William Sims each enjoyed two whisky and sodas. The party stayed at Mary Tavy for only about ten minutes before heading back to Tavistock, singing as they went. Witnesses saw the car driving along at a sensible and steady speed, which Gregory later stated was around fifteen miles an hour.

On Parkwood Road, just outside Kelly College in Tavistock, the car collided with a lamp post and overturned. Winnie Sims hit her head on the road and although her new husband managed to pull her from the damaged vehicle, she died almost instantly. Gregory sustained a serious shoulder injury and several broken ribs, while Joseph Craze also received a shoulder injury. Nellie and William were fortunate to escape with minor cuts and bruises.

An inquest was opened and adjourned, to allow Gregory and Craze time to recover in hospital before being called as witnesses. When it re-opened, coroner Mr R.R. Rodd was told that a motor engineer had been unable to pinpoint any particular mechanical defects in the car, which might have accounted for the accident, although he conceded that the steering joints of the car may have temporarily locked and then freed themselves on impact.

Percy Gregory, who was said to be a careful, experienced and skilful driver, who had never previously had a car accident, told the inquest that something had gone wrong with the steering. The vehicle had suddenly and unexpectedly pulled hard to the right and, when he tried to correct it, the steering locked.

Gregory said that he knew the road well and had already driven that way on the evening in question to take the rector home. He had drunk a single glass of wine during the day and, when asked by the coroner if he thought it prudent to have drunk two whisky and soda drinks in quick succession before driving, he explained that it was a very cold night. (Surprisingly the police seemed to support Gregory, telling the inquest that they had made enquiries into the matter and he was perfectly sober when admitted to hospital after the accident.)

The road was a notorious accident blackspot and, on the night of the accident, it was also covered in mud, which had frozen. It was suggested that the car may have hit a pot hole and with no other obvious explanation for the tragedy, the jury agreed on a verdict of 'accidental death'.

South East

Brighton, East Sussex

After proposing a toast to the bride and bridegroom at the wedding of his son, Percy to Elizabeth May Cole in March 1932, retired railway official Henry Matthews turned to his wife and asked 'How was that?'

'It was all right' she reassured him, at which her husband promptly fell down dead at her feet.

The bride and groom cancelled their planned honeymoon and went into mourning.

Staines, Middlesex

In February 1939, seventeen-year-old Doris Howard and her twenty-five-year-old brother, George, unwittingly arranged their weddings to take place at the same Registry Office within half an hour of each other. George, who married Dora Beckett, told contemporary newspapers that he and his sister were two of twelve children, who lived with their mother and stepfather in Ashford. He normally left the house to go to work before his sister and she was usually out when he returned home, so the siblings had little chance to chat about their respective plans. It was only when Doris told George that she was to be married the following week to James Llewellyn, that they realised the coincidence.

Dunsford, Surrey

An inquest was held on 19th August 1911 on the death of twenty-year-old carter Percy Edward Pleasance, who died on the eve of his wedding. He and his new wife had planned to move to Australia to begin farming there at the beginning of September.

Percy had told his father that he was going to bathe. His father had strongly advised him not to go alone, but Percy told him that he would be fine and was hardly likely to drown in eighteen inches of water. What he didn't realise was that the pond he had chosen for his swim had a huge hole in the middle, where the water was sixteen feet deep.

When Percy didn't return, his father went to look for him, finding his clothes on the bank. The pool was dragged but Percy's body was not recovered, so farmhand Richard Longley (or Langley) bravely went into the water and dived down several times looking for him without success. Percy's body was eventually recovered later that day.

At the inquest, the coroner commended Longley for his bravery and the jury returned a verdict of 'accidentally drowned'.

Note: Most contemporary newspapers give the deceased's surname as Plesance. Official records suggest Pleasance is the correct name.

Slough, Berkshire

Frederick William Cox had impregnated his twenty-year-old girlfriend, Miss Alice Walters, but had agreed to marry her. The wedding was arranged for 1 July 1922. The bride-to-be had left her job in anticipation of marriage and motherhood and, on the morning of the wedding, she and her bridesmaids were dressed in their best, awaiting that arrival of the groom at her parents' house, to go to Slough Registry Office for the ceremony.

Instead of the groom, a policeman arrived at the door with the sad news that Cox had been found hanged at his uncle's house in Cippenham Green. The bride was prostrate with grief and the wedding arrangements had to be quickly cancelled.

At the inquest on Cox's death, his uncle, with whom the deceased had lived for several years, related going to his nephew's room at eight o'clock on the morning of the wedding and finding it empty.

James Stanborough immediately began a search for his nephew, who was eventually found hanging by a clothes line from a beam in a shed, his feet barely touching a rabbit hutch that he had dragged from its normal place to allow him to reach the beam.

Twenty-three-year-old Cox and Miss Walters had been together for a year. On the day before their wedding, Cox had been at her house until eleven o'clock at night and had seemed perfectly normal, giving no indication that he intended to kill himself.

William Britton told the inquest that he had employed Cox as a causal labourer for the past three months, paying him twenty-seven shillings a week. According to Britton, Cox was always hard up, so much so that he had recently borrowed against his wages to purchase a dog licence.

Coroner Mr A. E. W. Charsley was scathing in his condemnation of Cox who '…got the young lady into trouble then committed this dastardly act to get out of facing his responsibilities.' He returned a verdict of *'felo de se'*, an archaic term for suicide committed when the deceased was judged to be of sound mind, which literally translates as 'felon of him or herself'.

Mitcham, Surrey

With their wedding arranged for 29th November 1930, on the evening of 27th November, twenty-one-year-old Winifred Gladys Block and her fiancé Alfred Charles Davis were doing some last-minute decorating on what was to be their marital home, helped by Winifred's father.

When Winifred began to feel unwell, her father went for a doctor, leaving Alfred sitting with his fiancée. Suddenly she cried out 'Help me, Alfie!' before collapsing. By the time her father arrived back with a doctor she was dead and it was later confirmed that, although

Winifred suffered from valvular heart disease of rheumatic origin, the actual cause of her death was a pulmonary embolism.

At an inquest held by East Surrey coroner Mr F.J. Nightingale, Davis collapsed with grief while giving evidence and had to be carried from the room. The inquest jury returned a verdict of 'natural death.'

Hounslow, Middlesex

On 27th May 1950, Miss Barbara Ogglesby and the wedding guests waited at St Mary's Church, Sunbury-on-Thames for the groom, Douglas Scott. When he didn't arrive, a search was initiated and he was later found in a coma in the Hounslow flat that was to be the couple's marital home. He died without regaining consciousness.

His fiancée visited the flat and found an empty bottle and syringe, which she handed to investigating officers. The residue in each was found to be a very concentrated solution of morphine, which was apparently home-made.

The cause of Scott's death was determined as morphia poisoning and he apparently possessed an ample supply of drugs and syringes, which he could easily have obtained while serving in the Army. At an inquest held by coroner Mr H. G. Broadbridge, Barbara Ogglesby stated that she had seen her fiancé on the night before the wedding, just after he had purchased the tickets for their honeymoon. She had noticed nothing out of the ordinary about his behaviour or demeanour.

The coroner told the jury that there was no suggestion that Scott had intended his own death. 'I am satisfied that it was not intentional' Broadbridge declared 'but, on the other hand, I cannot assume it was an accident'. The jury returned an open verdict.

Wraysbury, Buckinghamshire

At Windsor County Court on 22nd November 1926, accountant David Welsh sued solicitor Alton Leslie Pound for damages for injuries caused at Pound's wedding.

Welsh was a guest at the wedding and, after the reception at Wraysbury, the newlyweds set off on their honeymoon, in a car driven by the bridegroom. Welsh and another guest walked in front of the car for a little way, banging tin trays to give the couple a rousing send off. As the car accelerated slightly, the other guest stepped out of the way but Welsh claimed that he was taken by surprise and could not move out of the way fast enough. He told the court that he had rested on the starting handle and clung on to the headlights but had eventually fallen, turned a somersault and ended up wedged underneath the driver's seat with a dislocated hip and shoulder.

Pound stated that Welsh had deliberately climbed onto the front of the car and perched there like a mascot. He believed that, had he stopped the car, he would have been seen as not being a good sport but now, since he hadn't stopped the car, he was being blamed for the accident.

The judge ruled that any sensible person would have stopped the car when he saw a man sitting precariously on his radiator but Pound chose to carry on the joke by driving in the dark along a bumpy road, when it was more than likely that Welsh would fall off. Therefore, the joke was on him and he must have the pleasure of paying for it. Pound was fined £100 plus costs.

Sheerness, Kent

Thirty-seven-year-old Chief Petty Officer James Robert Marjoram married Elizabeth Martha Wood at Sheerness on 14th June 1899. The couple were enjoying their wedding reception with their guests when a Corporal from Marjoram's ship *H.M.S. Wildfire* arrived. Marjoram had absented himself without leave and the corporal had orders to escort him back to his ship.

Marjoram asked for, and was granted, permission to change out of his wedding finery into his uniform. He withdrew to another room and, moments later, a shot rang out and he lay dead.

Marjoram's suicide was obviously pre-planned, as he had hidden fifty bullets in the room and left three sealed letters, addressed to his new wife and his friends. The letter to his wife read: *'Good-bye darling. I am found out just in time. I am a married man. God forgive me. I hope we shall meet in heaven.'*

Nobody was more surprised by Marjoram's suicide than his real wife, Rosannah, who he married in 1885 and with whom he had two children. Mrs Marjoram stated that she had last seen her husband a month earlier, when he had come home on leave. According to Mrs Marjoram, their marriage was very happy and her husband was on the verge of leaving the navy so that he could live on his pension.

Eastleigh, Hampshire

Nineteen-year-old Annie Christine Palin was due to marry thirty-six-year-old retired major Stirling Windrop Stirling on 23rd December 1920. However, on the morning of the wedding, as a hairdresser arrived at her parents' house to do her hair, Annie slipped out of the back door with a suitcase, telling her parents that she wanted to put her luggage with her fiancé's. As the vicar and guests waited at Bitterne Congregational Church and a sumptuous meal for seventy guests was prepared for the reception, Annie apparently called briefly at the hotel where her fiancé was staying then disappeared.

Nothing was heard from her for two days until her parents received a telegram, which read *'All well. Writing. Annie.'* Since her parents did not receive the promised letter and knew no-one at Haslemere, from where the telegram was sent, they suspected it was a hoax.

Shortly before her wedding day, Annie had ordered a trousseau costing £320, paid for by her fiancé, who cancelled the cheque as soon as she failed to show up for their wedding.

As the days passed, it emerged that Annie had gone missing once before. She worked as a probationary nurse at the Work House in Epsom and, in August 1920, had told the Master there that she was going to London to meet her father. When she didn't return, the Master sent a telegram to her father, who knew of no arrangement to meet his daughter.

Annie's photograph was published in the contemporary newspapers and she was recognised by someone at Pulborough in Sussex. She returned home by taxi on 1st January 1921 and the only comment that she would give to the press was that she had changed her mind for private reasons and now had no intention of marrying her fiancé.

On leaving home, she had apparently found a taxi and told the driver to '...drive anywhere.' She ended up at Southampton West Station, where she left the first taxi and took another to Docks Station. Once there, she changed her mind again and asked to be driven to Northam Station, from where she took a slow train to London. She went from London to Liverpool, where she is reported to have stayed either with friends or with a married sister. From there she returned to Pulborough and then home.

Note: Some contemporary newspapers name the bridegroom as Stirling Westrop Stirling. His age is also given as twenty-two in some publications, but since his occupation is said to be a retired Army major, this seems unlikely.

Redhill, Surrey

Station Road, Redhill (author's collection)

Twenty-four-year-old Harry Edward Sharp managed a wine and spirits shop on Station Road, Redhill. He was due to marry Violet Ellen Freeman on 28th September 1929 and, early that morning, he went to the shop to hand over to the relief manager.

The errand should have taken no more than thirty minutes and, when Harry didn't arrive home at the expected time, his brother Frederick went to look for him. When he got to the shop, he found it still locked, with an errand boy waiting outside, unable to get in.

Frederick went back home for the spare set of keys and when he unlocked the shop, the first thing he saw was a pencilled note on the shop counter reading *'Beware of gas in cellar'*. Going downstairs, he found Harry lying dead on the floor, a rubber pipe leading to a gas fitting in his mouth and his head covered by his coat.

Although Harry was unresponsive, a Dr Crichton lived just a few doors away from the shop and quickly began artificial respiration, which he continued for almost thirty minutes before admitting defeat.

At an inquest held at the Cemetery Chapel, Reigate, Coroner Mr F. G. Nightingale was told that Harry had been happy to be getting married, although he had seemed rather 'excited' before leaving for the shop.

Harry's employer was called to give evidence and stated that, although Harry was a steady, sober and reliable manager, some small discrepancies had recently been found in his accounts and his branch was about to face an audit.

Harry was known as a very private person, who did not discuss his business with anybody. The coroner theorised that he was afraid that the detailed audit might expose the irregularities in his book-keeping and that he would not be able to explain where the missing money had gone. The inquest jury returned a verdict of 'suicide while of unsound mind', communicating their deepest sympathies to the dead man's fiancée, who attended the inquest dressed head to toe in black.

Note: Miss Freeman's middle name is variously given as Ellen, Eileen and Elizabeth in the contemporary newspapers.

Isle of Grain, Kent

Twenty-eight-year-old former sailor Stanley Know was due to be married on 7th August 1920. Having left home on 6th August to go and see his fiancée, he was never seen alive again and his body was found on 9th August floating in a creek at Isle of Grain.

He had two notes in his pockets, one addressed to his mother and the other to his fiancée. To his mother he wrote. *'It cannot be helped. I have got to do it. There is not a lot to live for, mother, only hard work.'* To his fiancée, he wrote: *'Good-bye Arty, I wish you were here so that I could kiss your dear face but I have your photo and I can kiss that. It is the photo of the girl I love better than life. I am going with it next to my heart. Well, my dear girl, my time is short. Go and see mother sometimes, she will be glad to see you. Try to find someone who will look after you better than I can.'*

The inquest on Know's death recorded a verdict of 'suicide while of unsound mind.'

Southend-on-Sea, Essex

Gas fitter Frederick William Bilz (24) regularly played at full back for his work's football team 'Gas Light and Coke Co.'

On 10th April 1937, Bilz was struck on the side of the head by a football. He carried on playing for the rest of the match without complaint, then went to work as normal for the next three days. However, on the fourth day after the match, he began to feel unwell and soon became confused and delirious. He was rushed to Southend Municipal Hospital, where he died on 17th April, almost exactly at the time when he should have been marrying Edith Mary Pond.

Pathologist Dr L. Bond performed a post-mortem examination and found that the deceased suffered from a latent nasal infection. Apparently, this was a common condition, which many people had without knowing anything about it. Yet on this occasion, the blow to his head had triggered a very rare reaction, leading to an acute infection and the cause of Bilz's death was given as septic meningitis.

At the inquest on his death, coroner Mr F. L. Beccle recorded a verdict of 'accidental death'.

Woodstock, Oxfordshire

On 3rd February 1923, war widow Mrs Lilian Mary Eary and George Edington married at the Registry Office at Woodstock. Until Mrs Eary arrived from London for their wedding, the couple had never actually met in person, having carried out their entire courtship by letter.

Rivenhall, Essex

On 6th December 1938, nine days before he was due to get married, Lieutenant Guy Bertram Streatfield Slater, who served aboard *H.M.S. Ganges,* attended his fiancée's birthday party in London. When Patricia Adams saw his train off from Liverpool Street Station, he told her that he was feeling very tired and that he hoped to get some sleep on the train. Slater was later found unconscious on the railway line at Rivenhall. He was taken to Chelmsford Hospital, where he subsequently died.

At an inquest on his death, Coroner Mr Beccle was told that Slater was normally a very fit, athletic man, who regularly played squash and Rugby and who very rarely drank alcohol. However, he had contracted dysentery in China, which often made him feel nauseous and abnormally tired. He was also suffering from an abscess on his liver. Pathologist Francis Camps, who conducted the post-mortem examination, confirmed the presence of the abscess, describing Slater as '...not at all a fit man' and attributing his death to shock and a fractured forehead.

A passenger on the train stated that he had seen a man '...who might or might not have been Slater' leave a compartment and walk along the train's corridor, towards the engine. Train guard Thomas George London later found a hat, coat and an attaché case bearing the initials G.B.S. in an empty compartment and, as London looked for their owner, he came across an open door, with a puddle of vomit nearby.

Patricia Adams made a statement, which was read at the inquest. She had been courting her fiancé for four years and they had been engaged for eleven months. 'We were both very happy' her statement concluded.

Coroner Mr Beccle told the inquest jury that there was no suggestion whatsoever of foul play. Slater had had a tiring and exciting day and was no doubt feeling exhausted. The likelihood was that he had fallen asleep in the train and woke up, feeling somewhat mentally confused, going to the train window either to vomit or for some fresh air and, in his confusion, opening the door and falling out. The inquest jury concurred, finding a verdict of 'accidental death.'

Hastings, Sussex

Miss Evelyn Cross and Mr Cyril Burton were married on 14th June 1925 and went to Hastings for their honeymoon, where they rented an apartment for a week.

On 20th June, Evelyn left the flat at a few minutes before eight o'clock in the morning, saying that she was going to get something for their breakfast. When she didn't return, Cyril went out to look for her and, when he couldn't find her, he reported her missing to the police.

Evelyn was found some hours later on a ledge, partway down a two-hundred-and-fifty-foot cliff and although she was still alive, she died on her way to hospital. Her hat and handbag were never found.

At the inquest on her death, her husband collapsed in tears when the coroner asked if he had identified his wife's body. He told the inquest that their honeymoon was going wonderfully well and, as far as he knew, his new bride was happy and had no worries. He confirmed that Evelyn had gone missing for a day before the wedding, during which she had just walked about, but attributed that to pre-wedding nerves.

Evelyn's father had received a letter from his daughter, sent from Hastings, in which she sounded very happy and seemed her usual cheerful self.

The inquest returned an open verdict, finding insufficient evidence to decide between accident or suicide.

Beaconsfield, Buckinghamshire

The wedding between Charles Samuel Witt and Emily Norris was scheduled to take place on 23rd September 1905. However, Witt's family disapproved of his choice of bride, who already had two illegitimate children, and so, in a fit of pique, instead of standing at the altar, Witt threw himself into the village pond.

He was rescued and brought before the Petty Sessions on 25th September, charged with attempting to commit suicide. Having fainted, he was discharged and, on leaving the court, was met by Miss Norris, who promptly hustled him to the church where they were married.

Although the couple went on to have a child together, their marriage did not last. In 1907, Witt was brought before magistrates, charged with failing to maintain his wife and family, leaving them the responsibility of Amersham Parish. Witt, who appeared in court in the uniform of the 4th Oxfordshire Light Infantry, was sentenced to one day in prison and advised to live up to his responsibilities.

Epping Green, Essex

There was only ever one woman for Charles Ricketts of Epping Green, Essex, and when he and his girlfriend Mary Ann Andrews parted, he was devastated when she married another man soon afterwards.

Ricketts remained a bachelor and when Mary Ann was widowed at seventy-eight-years-old, he quickly proposed marriage. By now, Mary Ann was blind in one eye and was said to be very feeble and a bit unsteady on her legs but none of that mattered to Ricketts.

Less than three weeks after their wedding in October 1905, Mary Ann was found dead in a pond behind the couple's house. There was a pail on the pond's bank and another in the pond.

At an inquest on her death, coroner Mr Lewis said that she had obviously overbalanced while trying to get water. Ricketts admitted that his new wife had already fallen into the pond three times before and the inquest jury returned a verdict of 'accidental death.'

Brentford, Middlesex

In November 1905, Ellen Louisa Taint (nee Brown) went to Brentford Police Court to sue her husband Frederick for maintenance. Frederick denied the fact that he and Ellen were legally married, telling the court that they had both been so drunk on their wedding day that the vicar had thrown them out of the church.

Ellen's brother, Thomas, was called to give evidence. He explained that he, Ellen and another girl went to church on Easter Monday 1896 for the purpose of getting married. 'We were all drunk and somehow we seemed to get mixed up' he explained. 'I gave away the girl I was going to marry to someone else and my girl gave away Fred Taint. After a bit, we all got properly married but when we were signing the register Fred told the vicar 'I suppose you reckon yourself a better man than your father at this game but you ain't.'' At this, the vicar got rather angry, told Taint to be quiet and asked them all to leave.

The Bench found that the ceremony was legal and hearing that Taint had paid his wife only a single penny in the last five months, awarded her a separation order and 19s a week maintenance.

Birchington-on-Sea, Kent

On 8th November 1932, Jane Mary Davies left her aunt's home in Ilford, Essex, where she had been staying to meet her fiancé, William David Phillips, at Liverpool Street Station. She never arrived for the appointment nor did she return to her aunt's house and Phillips quickly reported her missing to the local police.

The couple were due to marry on 10th November, but Jane didn't return for the wedding.

Almost a week later, a woman was walking through Birchington-on-Sea in Kent, when she happened to notice that a holiday home owned by her uncle had a broken window. She mentioned this to her father, who wrote to Mr. S.G. Birdseye to notify him of the damage to his property. Birdseye contacted a firm of estate agents and asked them to arrange to have the window repaired.

When clerk Bernard Rayner went to the property, he noticed that there was a footprint on the draining board under the broken window. Looking round the rest of the house, he was horrified to discover a woman hanging by a length of electrical cord from the bannisters.

The police were notified and, on searching the other rooms, they found a woman's hat, shoes and handbag in one of the bedrooms. The handbag contained letters, papers relating to a wedding and a bankbook identifying her as the missing bride-to-be from Ilford.

At an inquest held on her death by coroner Mr E.T. Lambert, the chief witnesses were Jane's cousin and her fiancé.

Her cousin stated that Jane was susceptible to attacks of nerves and had suffered a nervous breakdown the previous year. However, he believed that she was looking forward to her wedding, adding that she and Phillips were devoted to each other and very much in love. Two marriage licenses had been taken out for their wedding. Apparently, after getting married, the couple had planned a honeymoon in Bournemouth before moving to London, where they were going to open a small dairy. Having taken out the first license, they realised that it wouldn't permit them to marry until after the date on which they were due to take up their shop, so they decided to take out a special license to give themselves time for a honeymoon before venturing into business.

Phillips stated that he was aware that his fiancée suffered with her nerves, adding that she was inclined to worry about the smallest thing. 'She was queer the day before I saw her last' he admitted, although he added that he had never expected that she would try to take her own life.

Jane had once holidayed in Birchington, although she was not familiar with the property where she was found, neither was there any connection between her and its owner, Mr Birdseye.

The inquest jury returned a verdict of 'suicide while of unsound mind.'

Ardley, Oxfordshire

The wedding of thirty-three-year-old farmer and Post Office keeper William Addison (a.k.a. Cooke) and twenty-three-year-old Rose Jane Beasley of Ardley was arranged for 16th August 1905. The couple had been courting for more than five years and were always said to be on the most affectionate terms with each other.

On the night before the wedding, Rose went to see William's married sister, Clara, to invite her to attend the celebrations. William arrived at the house a little later, then Rose's parents. It was then that William confessed that the wedding would have to be postponed for a few days, since it had not proved possible to get the certificate of banns in time for the ceremony to take place as planned. Everyone was disappointed – William's mother and sister told him that he shouldn't have left it to the last minute to sort things out, while Rose's mother, who had already prepared the wedding breakfast for the following day, was understandably annoyed and told the couple that she would have nothing more to do with the wedding if it had to be postponed.

Before the Beasleys went home, Rose and William were allowed a little privacy to say their goodnights outside. They had barely left the house, when the sound of groaning was heard. Mrs Beasley went outside to see what was going on and was horrified to see William kneeling over Rose, sawing at her throat with a razor.

Ann Beasley flung herself at William, grabbed his coat and tried to pull him away from her daughter. Without speaking, William stood up and punched Ann in the face, stunning her so that she let go of his coat. Immediately her hold was released, William bolted.

Ann's screams brought people rushing from the cottage to help Rose and, as she was being led back indoors, William suddenly leaped the garden wall and threw himself at her again, knocking her over. He was seized by his father and a neighbour but while he was being frogmarched into the house, the neighbour stumbled and William broke free. Seizing an iron bar, he ran to the Beasleys' home, where, believing Rose to be inside, he began smashing windows. He then ran back to his sister's house and smashed windows there, before making off into nearby woods.

A doctor was called to attend to Rose and found that, although her throat had been cut from ear to ear, the eight-inch long cut had miraculously missed all of the major blood vessels. Eighteen stitches were placed in her neck, along with a further seven to reattach the top part of her ear, which had been almost severed in the attack.

William was caught the following day and was arrested and charged with Rose's attempted murder. By the time the case reached the Assizes, the charges against him were 'feloniously wounding with intent to murder', with a second lesser charge of 'unlawful wounding.'

Fortunately, Rose survived the attack against her and was able to give evidence at William's trial. She stated that William had written to her from Oxford Prison, apologising for what he had done and placing the blame for his actions on Rose's parents, particularly her mother for the way she spoke to him. He signed the letter '...*from your loving young man, William Cook*' adding around twenty x's to represent kisses. Rose failed to understand how William could place any blame on her parents, who had provided most of the furniture for the couple's marital home. She told the court that, although William professed himself to be keen to get married, he had seemed to take little interest in the arrangements and had left things like furnishing the house entirely to her. Right up until the very moment he attacked her, William had been his usual, affectionate self, although with hindsight, she now felt that he had a bit of a strange look in his eyes all evening.

William pleaded 'not guilty', telling the court that he was '...very, very sorry – truly sorry - for what I have done.' He swore that he had never had any intention of hurting his fiancée, adding that the razor with which he cut her throat was in his pocket because he had taken it to be sharpened.

The jury found William guilty of the lesser count of unlawful wounding and he was sentenced to fifteen months' imprisonment, with hard labour. Apparently, he was still very keen to marry Rose – she was understandably less keen and records show that she married another man in 1914.

Near Whitstable, Kent

In February 1860, Frederick Kemp left Whitstable in a carriage drawn by two horses for his wedding in Canterbury. After the ceremony, he and his bride, Fanny Austin, enjoyed a reception and left Canterbury at nine o'clock using the same carriage and horses, which they had agreed to share with two of the wedding guests.

It had been snowing heavily during the day and the roads were rapidly becoming impassable. Roughly two miles before Whitstable, the carriage driver pulled up and told his passengers that he was unable to proceed any further. Ignoring their protests, he unhitched the horses and led them back to Whitstable, leaving the wedding party to spend the night in the freezing cold carriage. It was not until nine o'clock the following morning that they were rescued.

Southend-on-Sea, Essex

On 8th October 1927, police were alerted to a man's hat and overcoat, which had apparently been abandoned on the pier at Southend-on-Sea. On searching the area, they soon found a man's body in the sea.

The Pier, Southend-on-Sea (author's collection)

Papers in the coat pockets identified the deceased as Charles Thomas Read, a widower with one child, who worked as the manager of the Chatham branch of the International Tea Company Stores Ltd. There was also a doctor's letter dated 4th October, certifying that he was unable to work due to neurasthenia and papers pertaining to his wedding to Miss Doris Weller, which should have taken place that very day.

A postcard was found clutched in Read's hand when his body was pulled from the water. The message on it read: *'Dearest Doris, my* head won't let me come home. I am longing for you and I am taking you with me forever. You are the sweetest. Try and forget me. I am heartbroken, Love Charles xxx'

A second note was found on the pier, which read: *'Dearest, what shall I do? My back is breaking, my head too. I cannot stick it much longer. I seem to be wandering. I see miles of water but how I got here I don't know. It is calling me and I must go. So goodbye and with best love. Please don't let anyone wear black or send flowers for I am not good enough. I can see your face in the water. Goodbye, I cannot be a worry to you all your life xxx'.*

Southend coroner Mr H.J. Jeffries held an inquest on Read's death, at which it was revealed that the deceased suffered not only from neurasthenia but also from rheumatism and was in severe pain most of the time. Although he had undoubtedly been looking forward to marrying the woman he loved, the fact that he was unable to work because of his illness obviously weighed heavily on his mind and hence he took his own life rather than be a burden to his fiancée.

The inquest returned a verdict of 'suicide during temporary insanity.'

Worplesden, Surrey

On Wednesday 30th August 1899, a man deliberately threw himself in front of a train at Worplesden Station near Woking. The train was travelling at fifty miles an hour and the man's terribly mangled body was carried for almost 100 yards. The deceased was later identified as thirty-five-year-old gardener George Withall and it emerged that the day of his death should have been his wedding day.

George left behind a note for his fiancée, Miss Elizabeth Smith:

'Dear Lizzie, please forgive me for what I have done but really I could not show my face in Chobham any more. I hope and trust that you will get through this trouble. What I have done this for I do not know but the sooner I do away with myself, the better it will be for all. I feel quite myself again now. I am too far away from home to be able to get back for our wedding. Such a vagabond as I am is not worth troubling about. I do however hope and trust that you will forgive me after I am gone. I should like to see you again but you know I have treated you most awfully cruel. How could I show myself in Chobham again? I do not deserve your sympathy, for had I taken your advice, I should now be happy and comfortable, whereas I am obliged to take my life through my own disgrace. Good-bye! May the Lord help you out of your trouble.'

Nobody could understand the 'disgrace' referred to in Withall's letter. At the inquest, which was held at Worplesden Railway Station, a police officer told coroner Mr G.F. Roumieu that he knew of no trouble concerning the deceased, adding that Withall had already made all of the arrangements for his forthcoming wedding and furnished a house ready to receive his new bride.

Joseph Turner of Cobham knew Withall and his family well. He last saw him the day before his death, at which time Withall appeared very strange in his manner. He mentioned that he was going to be married the following day but cried bitterly, saying that he did not intend to return in time for the ceremony. Turner thought Withall seemed deranged and was so concerned about him that he immediately telegraphed Withall's father, William.

William told the inquest that his son had recently suffered from sunstroke and had complained of having a bad head. Other than that, he could think of no reason whatsoever why his son might have taken his own life. The inquest jury returned a verdict of 'suicide whilst of unsound mind.'

Dagenham, Essex

An unusual wedding took place at St Martin's Church, Dagenham, on 24th October 1936.

In a double ceremony, Matthew Clark married widow Mrs Hannah Clark and Hannah's eldest son, Lionel Clark, married Matthew's daughter, Alice Clark.

Lionel gave away his mother, then acted as best man to his prospective father-in-law. Mr Clark senior then gave away his daughter and acted as his future son-in-law's best man.

Horsted Keynes, Sussex

After their wedding at Horsted Parish Church on 31st July 1943, Gunner Ronald Knapp and Winifred Ellen Standing went to the bride's father's farmhouse for the reception.

When the wedding breakfast was over, the newlyweds escorted Ronald's parents to the bus stop, where they waved them off on their journey home to Haywards Heath, before setting off to walk back to the farm.

Shortly afterwards, a train that pulled into Horsted Keynes Station was seen to have a torn mackintosh coat on the front buffers. An immediate search of the railway line was launched and Mr and Mrs Knapp were found lying by the rails – he was dead, she was barely breathing and died within minutes.

At a double inquest held by coroner Dr E.F. Hoare, much was made of the fact that there was no level crossing on the railway line anywhere near where the Knapps were found, and they had therefore been guilty of trespassing. There was a heavy thunderstorm at the time of the accident, and it was suggested that the couple were running and holding their raincoats over their heads when they took an illicit shortcut home and thus neither saw nor heard the train that hit them.

The coroner returned verdicts of 'accidental death' on the couple, exonerating the train driver from any blame.

Nettlestead, Kent

After returning from work on 4th October 1929, twenty-eight-year-old bricklayer Edward Cornelius Adams went to his parents' henhouse to tend to the chickens. Soon afterwards, a neighbour noticed smoke coming from the wooden shed and within a very short time the whole building was consumed by flames.

Neighbours fought to put out the fire, never suspecting that there was anyone inside the hut. It was only when Adams's parents arrived that they were told that he was there but by then the flames were too intense for anyone to attempt a rescue. When the fire was eventually extinguished, his body was recovered from the ashes of the building.

Adams had been engaged for two years and was due to marry twenty-three-year-old Eva Symonds from a neighbouring village the next morning. She was prostrate with grief when told of her fiancé's death, particularly since it fell to her to identify him from his engagement ring, since he was so charred and blackened by the fire that his features were unrecognisable.

The Hop Pole Inn, Nettlestead (author's collection)

Coroner Mr A. H. Neve held an inquest at the Hop Pole Inn, Nettlestead, at which it was stated that Adams had died from a combination of burns and shock. There was a can of petrol in the hen house – ironically it was kept there rather than at the house for safety. When Adams was found, the petrol can was by his side and its screw top had been removed. What little that remained of Adams's clothes were soaked in a mixture of petrol and water.

Nobody at the inquest could believe that Adams had deliberately taken his own life. He was a jovial man, who had made all of the preparations for his wedding and was looking forward to starting life as a married man. A doctor who testified at the inquest stated that Adams was known to be a smoker and there could have been petrol vapour in the hen house that was ignited by his lighted cigarette. The neighbours who tried to put out the fire stated that the shed door was not locked. It opened outwards and could easily have been pushed open from inside.

The coroner told the jury that he didn't believe that Adams had gone to the hen house with the deliberate intention of doing away with himself and accordingly the jury returned a verdict of 'accidental death'.

Maidenhead, Berkshire

On 30th May 1925, Grace Muriel Robey waited at the altar of St Luke's Church, Maidenhead, for the arrival of her groom. When Daniel Cecil Kimpton didn't arrive, a search was made for him but it wasn't until the following morning that his decapitated body was found at Wallham Siding on the Great Western Railway, roughly four miles from the church where he should have married. By the side of the railway line lay a brand-new gold wedding ring in its box and a receipt for the wedding cake was in one of Kimpton's pockets.

An inquest on Kimpton's death was opened on 2nd June but immediately adjourned for one week, since Miss Robey was too distressed to attend. When the inquest reopened, Kimpton's landlady told the coroner that Kimpton's new suit had been laid out on his bed ready for the ceremony. Kimpton had left the house on the morning of the wedding intending to get a haircut, but had never returned.

The landlady revealed that she had seen Kimpton and his fiancée the night before the wedding, when both looked unwell and miserable. 'You look as if you're going to a funeral rather than a wedding' she told them.

Miss Robey stated that she and Kimpton had been engaged for two years and that they had both been looking forward to married life. They went up to London a few days before the wedding to buy furniture for the rooms where they intended to make their marital home and Kimpton told her that he had paid a deposit of £10 and that the furniture would be delivered before the wedding. Two days later, they bought the wedding ring and paid for the cake.

A cousin of Kimpton's revealed that on the night before the wedding, Kimpton told him that he was '...in a tight corner' and tried to borrow £5 or £6. The couple's furniture had still not arrived at their rooms and, unbeknown to Miss Robey, Kimpton had only paid £2 deposit and had not found a guarantor for the remaining outstanding money.

'This was a man who had reached the end of his tether' surmised the coroner. Kimpson had withdrawn all but 4s 2d from his bank account and the purchase of the wedding cake had used up all of his ready cash. Unable to face the shame of not providing a suitable home for his new bride, he had simply committed suicide rather than get married.

The inquest jury found a verdict of 'suicide whilst of unsound mind.'

Note: There are numerous variations in reported details in this case. In some contemporary newspapers, Miss Robey is named Miss Robey Furze Platt while Kimpton is variously named Daniel Cecil or David Cecil Kimpton or Kempton. According to official records, Daniel Cecil Kimpton seems to be the correct name.

Birchington-on-Sea, Kent

On February 28th 1933, Reverend William Fairclough was due to marry widow Margaret Helena Trillo at Birchington-on-Sea. However, sadly, Fairclough had a heart attack on the morning of the wedding and died two days later.

Mrs Trillo sent the couple's wedding cake to the Workhouse at Thanet, for the enjoyment of the aged female inmates.

'I feel sure he would have liked it to be used in this way and so would I' she explained.

Kingston-Upon-Thanes, Surrey

At around midnight on 28th May 1939, twenty-two-year-old John Alfred Wickham was driving his fiancée and her brother home from an outing to the country when his car suddenly swerved and hit a tree, partially overturning. Miss Gertrude Estelle Lynn and her brother, Albert, were thrown out of the car, fortunately landing on soft ground. Wickham however was trapped under the vehicle.

All three were taken to Kingston County Hospital, where Wickham died soon after admission. The news of his death was initially kept from Gertrude, who spent an uncomfortable night deliriously calling out his name.

Albert was discharged from hospital after treatment and, at the inquest on Wickham's death, he stated that the car was being driven properly when it had suddenly and unexpectedly swerved. His evidence was corroborated by two pedestrians who had witnessed the accident.

Wickham was a motor driver by profession and was known as an experienced and careful driver. Pathologist Dr E.T. Ruston told the coroner that his death was due to crushing injuries to his chest and the jury returned a verdict that Wickham died from injuries received in the accident but added that there was not enough evidence to show how the accident happened.

Gertrude and Wickham were due to get married on the 29th May and news of the tragedy was broken to the guests as they arrived for the ceremony.

Maidstone, Kent

On 14 July 1916, police called at a house in Maidstone in response to a telegram from Army authorities and Private William Edwards (45) of the Army Service Corps was arrested for being absent without leave from his wartime posting in France. Edwards maintained that he had a good reason to be A.W.O.L. – his wedding to widow Ellen Bowler was scheduled to take place at St Luke's Church, Maidenhead, at nine o'clock that morning and he had no intentions of missing it.

The police were sympathetic. Edwards was allowed to go to the church under police escort and he and Ellen were married, with Police Sergeant Humphreys actually acting as best man. After the ceremony, he was taken back to the police station, where he appeared before magistrates, who ordered his detention until transport could be arranged to take him back to France. His bride was allowed to visit him and there was what contemporary newspapers described as '...an affectionate parting.'

London

Mile End

Miss Eliza Ann Thompson was due to marry her fiancé, David Church (or Churches), on the morning of 15th October 1862. After putting on her wedding dress at home, she went into the parlour to show it to her father, Richard, who became very excited and almost immediately dropped to the floor.

Eliza screamed and her fiancé rushed into the room and lifted her unconscious father onto a chair. A doctor was sent for but Richard was beyond help, dying some four hours later aged just fifty.

At a later inquest, Dr Tainton told coroner Mr H. Raffles Walthew that death had resulted from effusion on the brain, produced no doubt by the excitement consequent on seeing his daughter in her bridal dress. The inquest jury returned a verdict that Richard Thompson died from apoplexy from excitement.

His daughter's wedding was postponed until 9th November 1862, when the ceremony apparently went off without further problems.

Camden Town

Twenty-five-year-old domestic cook Mary O'Brien and William Hoare had been courting for six months and their wedding was arranged for 23rd July 1932. The bride, bridegroom and their guests turned up at the church but there was no sign of the vicar and, when her brother made enquiries, he found that William had actually cancelled the wedding. Although William Hoare was waiting at the church, he said nothing at all about this, claiming ignorance when challenged.

It was agreed that the wedding would take place on 13th August and the wedding party went to the home of Brodie Hoare, William's sister. There was an argument between Hoare and Mary, who stormed out, after which Hoare was seen swigging from a blue glass bottle. His sister immediately dashed it from his hand and it shattered. When William O'Brien saw his sister at around five o'clock that afternoon, Mary told her brother that Hoare had left the country and gone to Tralee in Ireland.

That evening, Brodie saw Mary on a bus. Mary told her that her employer had given her some money and she was going on holiday to Brighton. Instead, she rented a room in Camden Town, where she was later found unconscious. Rushed to hospital, she recovered sufficiently to tell doctors that she had taken spirits of salts and mumbled '...going to be married this morning' and '...having a baby'.

Mary died later that night and at an inquest held on her death by coroner Mr Bentley Purchase, Hoare stated that he had asked Mary if they might postpone their wedding for two weeks and she had agreed. 'I was not in a position to marry', Hoare stated. 'I had no home to offer her and no work.'

'Hoare's explanation in the witness box does not fill me with a great amount of faith in him. It is clear that the girl did not think she was ever going to marry him' commented the coroner, as the jury found a verdict of 'suicide while of unsound mind'.

King's Cross

After their wedding on 19th March 1910, barman Henry George Ryan (25) and chambermaid Mary 'Kate' Martha Durrant (24) intended to go to Canada to live and had booked their passage for 23rd March. As they awaited the date of their departure, they rented rooms in Argyle Street, King's Cross.

They asked the landlady to give them a wake up call on the morning after the wedding but there was no response to her knocks on their door. Eventually, she went into their bedroom and found both Mr and Mrs Ryan lying dead in bed, dressed in their nightclothes. Both had apparently been dead for some time. The bride was laid out almost formally, her hands crossed in front of her so that her wedding ring was clearly visible. The groom had a piece of rag stuffed in his mouth. Mysteriously, three photographs had been propped up against the dressing table mirror – on the left, a portrait of Ryan, on the right a portrait of Mrs Ryan and in the middle a portrait of a young lady.

There were three letters in the room, one addressed to the coroner, one to the bride's mother and one to the bridegroom's father. The letter to the coroner read; *'This is not a case as it first appears to be of two persons agreeing to take poison together but one of murder and suicide by poison. I put the poison into her beer unseen by her. I watched her drink and waited for the consequences. We were sitting on the bed. I placed my arms around her to prevent her falling as I knew the end was coming in a few moments. After a short pang, she died suddenly without a struggle, almost with a sigh, merely closing her eyes as one who was weary, quiet and peaceable, very sweet and tender and looks now, as she lies, like one asleep. I write this to make less mystery of it. I have a reason for committing this mad act but I shall not disclose it. No blame should be attached to the girl. She was entirely under my influence and absolutely innocent of my intentions.'*

To Mrs Durrant, Ryan wrote: *'I am sorry to bring this trouble on you, but it had to be. Look after Kate's things and see that you get them all. The landlady is paid up. No money owing to anybody'* He then went on to quote Sydney Carton, adding; *'It is a far, far better thing that I do than I have ever done; it is a far, far better rest that I go to than I have ever known'*.

At an inquest held at St Pancras Coroner's Court, Mr and Mrs Durrant stated that they had learned of their daughter and son-in-law's deaths by reading about them in the newspaper. They were both fond of Ryan but had not attended the wedding because their daughter had not told them the time of the ceremony. They had received a letter from her apologising for not letting them know and promising to come to tea with them on the afternoon of 20th March.

The cause of the couple's death was confirmed as poisoning by Prussic Acid and a doctor called to their rooms by the landlady told the inquest that he had found a bottle labelled 'Syrup of Phosphate – a free trial bottle', which contained sufficient Prussic Acid to kill six people.

Coroner Dr Danford Thomas told the inquest jury that the woman in the centre portrait had not yet been identified. The inquest jury returned verdicts of wilful murder and suicide on the two deaths.

Shoreditch

On 7th November 1911, Mr John Forrester sued pastry cook Mr L. V. Durham for the sum of £3 10s, relating to damage to a wedding cake.

Forrester's daughter married in September 1911 and her mother made a three-tier wedding cake, which was sent to Durham for icing. Everyone was very happy with the result until the cake was cut at the wedding reception.

The top two tiers fell to pieces, most of which landed on the floor and it was impossible to cut a slice. The bride burst into tears and Mrs Forrester was so embarrassed that she had to leave the room' I was so humiliated I couldn't bear the sight of it' she told the court. On closer inspection, the Forresters believed that the bottom tier was Mrs Forrester's home-baked rich fruit cake and the top two tiers had been substituted with an inferior cake.

The Forresters told the court that the value of the top two tiers of the cake was thirty-five shillings, the remainder of their claim being for the bride's 'mental suffering'.

'I cannot assess tears and embarrassment, only tiers' said Judge Cluer.

Durham categorically denied having substituted the top tiers of the cake. 'Improper mixing would cause unequal distribution of air cells and the colour and texture might be entirely changed' he explained, adding 'This was an amateur made cake and the result is not altogether to be wondered at.'

The judge decided that it was more likely that a blunder had been made in the mixing of the cake than that Durham should be guilty of such a mean fraud, finding in favour of Durham.

Piccadilly

Thirty-three-year-old timber merchant and wharfinger Moses Goldman had lived at The Regent Palace Hotel for almost three years but was about to leave in order to get married to a Miss Fenton. However, on the morning of his wedding, he fell eighty feet to his death from the window of his hotel bedroom.

An inquest was held on his death on 2nd July 1920. The dead man's brother, Benjamin, described his brother's relationship with his fiancée, saying 'You couldn't meet a more

united couple'.

Moses apparently earned £1000 a year (equivalent to around £45,000 at today's rates) and had no worries. A house had been bought and furnished, the wedding and reception were planned and paid for and a honeymoon had been booked in Eastbourne.

The hotel manager told the inquest that the door to Goldman's bedroom had been locked from the inside and the dressing table had been moved slightly, in order to gain access to the window. The lower sash was open about twenty-nine inches and it was impossible for Goldman to fall out, although he could have leaned out and overbalanced.

Chamber maid Mary Cox had seen Goldman that morning and said that he seemed agitated and worried. He had eaten no breakfast and refused her offer of a cup of tea, poring over his Hebrew Bible and trembling.

Benjamin Goldman explained that it was the Jewish tradition for a bridegroom not to eat before his wedding and that Goldman could well have been revising the prayers he would be expected to recite at the ceremony. However, Mary Cox seemed to think that Moses Goldman's personality had changed over the previous two months, adding that he had mentioned business worries to her but not gone into any details.

A wedding ring had been found next to Goldman's body and his family strongly believed that he had been sitting by the window playing with it and dropped it, overbalancing as he tried to catch it. They were unaware of any business or financial worries and could think of no possible reason why Moses might have deliberately jumped from his eighth-floor window.

Regent's Palace Hotel (author's collection)

Coroner Mr Ingleby Oddie told the jury that Moses Goldman did not have venereal disease, which was apparently a frequent cause of suicide on the eve of marriage. The jury eventually returned an open verdict, stating that there was insufficient evidence to conclude whether Goldman's death was suicide or accidental.

Buckingham Palace / Chelsea / Aberdeen

At 2.00 a.m. on 30th April 1929, signaller George Edward Scott Sivewright of the 1st Scots Guards began a period of sentry duty outside Buckingham Palace. An hour later, a policeman on his beat noticed that his Sivewright's sentry box was unmanned and a little later a busby and a rifle were found in Green Park.

Nothing was seen of Sivewright until 11th May 1929, when he turned up at his home in Aberdeen, having walked almost 600 miles. After talking with his parents and his fiancée, Sivewright handed himself in to the police and was taken back to London to face a court martial, charged with leaving his post before he was relieved and with desertion from the Army by absenting himself without leave.

The court martial was held at Chelsea Barracks, where nineteen-year-old Sivewright explained that he had enlisted two years earlier and had been a keen and enthusiastic soldier, reaching the rank of Lance Corporal before, in his words 'I got entangled with a woman and drink.'

Although engaged to be married to a woman back in Scotland, Sivewright was unable to resist the other woman's charms and first went A.W.O.L. on 17th April. 'I lost my stripe because of her' he explained.

He was given three days of confinement to barracks and then, since he was due to be married at the end of April, he absented himself for an hour, intending to break off all relations with the other woman. Unfortunately for Sivewright, his absence was discovered and led to a further three days of confinement to barracks, meaning that he was unable to travel to Scotland for his wedding.

Sivewright told the court martial that he remembered going on duty on 30th April, then remembered nothing more until he found himself in Piccadilly. Too afraid to return to his post, he hung around the docks for a couple of days, hoping to get a passage to Aberdeen and, when this was unsuccessful, he walked the entire distance home.

The ruling of the court martial was that Sivewright should be discharged from the Army with ignominy and be sentenced to one hundred- and twelve-days' hard labour.

Sivewright eventually married a woman from Buckinghamshire in 1929. In 1934, he was again in trouble, charged with stealing property worth £18 4s 1½d from Metropolitan and Great Central Railway and also with stealing a policeman's bicycle, on which he made his getaway. His excuse that he had a slight difference of opinion with his wife and was in a temper at the time was not appreciated by the magistrates at Buckingham Police Court, who sentenced him to a total of three months' hard labour. The Station Master at Quainton, from where the money and goods were stolen, was Sivewright's father-in-law.

Southwark

On 24th July 1911, Southwark coroner Dr Waldo held an inquest on the death of forty-seven-year-old plasterer Horace Lambert, who was killed in a road accident while going to buy a wedding cake for his daughter's forthcoming marriage.

Witnesses stated that Horace stepped straight off the kerb in Walworth Road into the path of a bus and was knocked down.

Bus driver James Pitt denied that the bus mounted the kerb and hit Horace as he was waiting to cross the road and his evidence was corroborated by the bus conductor and several passengers.

The inquest jury returned a verdict of 'accidental death...due to apathy on the part of the deceased.' They exonerated the driver from any blame, adding that they though it would be an excellent idea if children were taught in school how to cross roads. According to the jury, this would waste more public money but might save some lives.

Whitehall

On 13th August 1927, twenty-three-year-old Esther Gordon was one of six bridesmaids at the wedding of her brother, Reuben, and his fiancée, Annie Mossbaum. After the ceremony at the Jewish Synagogue, the wedding party went to a hall in Whitechapel, where there was a lavish reception for around two hundred guests.

At around half-past eleven at night, with the festivities still in full swing, Esther felt ill and quickly fell unconscious. Her collapse triggered a bout of mass hysteria among the wedding guests, with many of the women screaming and fainting. Two women eventually required hospital treatment and several more had to be taken home by cab.

Meanwhile, an ambulance was called for Esther and she was rushed to the London Hospital. Although she was given oxygen on the way, on arrival at the hospital, she was pronounced dead.

House physician Dr A. C. Gardiner told the inquest on her death that Esther suffered from valvular disease of the heart, her condition so severe that she might have died at any time. None of her friends or family were aware of this and, in Gardiner's opinion, the excitement of the wedding feast was simply too much for her.

The inquest recorded a verdict of 'death from natural causes.'

Note: In some accounts, Esther's forename is given as Effie or Hettie. Official records seem to indicate that her given forename was Esther.

Bethnal Green

On 16th December 1883, Louisa Howse (or House) married William Crudgington. After leaving the church, they walked home to Little Collingwood Street to find Louisa's sister, Rosetta, and a crowd of her friends at their door, banging on saucepans, kettles and tin trays.

The newlyweds ignored the clamour and forced their way into the house. When the rowdy group refused to disperse, William opened the door and threw a bucket of cold water over them, at which they finally left.

However, the group reassembled later that evening and began banging again. Now Rosetta had armed herself with a poker, with which she hammered on her sister's door. When Louisa opened the door to tell everyone to go away, Rosetta hit her over the head with the poker, blacking her eye and cutting her forehead.

Rosetta was charged with assault and brought before magistrates at Worship Street Police Court. There she denied hitting her sister, claiming that Louisa had fallen over before her wedding. Asked why she was making such a din outside her sister's house, Rosetta claimed that it was done as '…a little rejoice', in the hope that the newlyweds might treat them to a drink.

Magistrates sentenced her to fourteen days imprisonment, commenting that it was a strange way in which to celebrate a wedding.

Marble Arch

On 24th October 1922, The Honourable Rosamund Bateman-Hanbury went to the Church of the Annunciation on Bryanston Street for her marriage to Hamilton A. Douglas Hamilton. As her wedding car arrived, a taxi pulled up outside the church porch and another bride emerged, looking radiant in a white and silver brocade dress with a white tulle veil, topped with a silver tiara.

The woman seemed in a trance and didn't appear to know where she was or what she was doing when questioned by the wedding guests. Eventually the police were called and she was put in another taxi and driven away. The only words she spoke while at the church were 'I am so sorry. I appear to be too late. I had hoped to get here first.'

The first taxi driver, who hadn't been paid for his journey, told police that he had picked up the woman in Sloane Street and driven her to Weatherby Mansions in Earl's Court, where she asked him to wait while she changed her clothes. When she got back into the cab dressed in her wedding finery, she urged the driver to hurry to the church as she didn't want to be late.

Once the mystery bride had gone, the wedding went ahead without further hitch. The interloper's identity was never discovered, although it was reported that she had appeared at least once before at another London church.

Regent's Canal

On 15th May 1880, sixty-six-year-old Sarah Small was at home in West Hampstead preparing for her daughter Elizabeth's wedding to Charles Maskell the next day. At around half-past ten at night, Sarah left the house and never returned. Her body was pulled from Regent's Canal the following morning.

At an inquest on her death held by coroner Dr Hardwicke, the jury heard that Sarah was a particularly sober woman. When she left home, she was carrying a purse containing a number of gold and silver coins, which was never found.

The inquest jury were initially unable to reach a unanimous decision but eventually returned an open verdict, leaving the police to investigate further. There is no evidence that a satisfactory explanation for Sarah's death was ever found.

Tragically, when Sarah was pulled from the canal dead, she was carried to the mortuary on the shoulders of four policemen. On their way, they met the wedding party returning from the church and the bride recognised her mother's corpse by her distinctive shawl.

Upper Holloway

On Boxing Day night 1932, forty-year-old restaurant car conductor Herbert William Patrick arrived at his sister's house drunk and tried to force his way in. His brother-in-law, Frederick John Webber, who had married Patrick's sister Nellie only that afternoon, tried to prevent him from coming in, telling him 'For God's sake go away. We don't want any trouble here.'

Patrick wouldn't see reason and continued to try and barge into the house. He and Webber scuffled and fell to the floor together. Patrick was picked up unconscious and later died.

At an inquest on his death, Webber told the coroner that he had no idea how they came to fall over. He swore that no blows had been exchanged between the two men.

Pathologist Sir Bernard Spilsbury had performed a post-mortem examination and cited the cause of Patrick's death as haemorrhage, consequent on a fracture of the skull. It was Spilsbury's contention that the pattern of bruising suggested that at least one blow had been struck, although Webber continued to insist that this had not happened.

Returning a verdict of 'accidental death', the coroner ruled that 'In law a man is entitled to put a man out of his house using whatever force is necessary. A man is entitled to the privacy of his own house'.

However, the coroner did add that if the death had happened in the street rather than a private house, the verdict might conceivably have been one of manslaughter.

Limehouse

Immediately prior to his wedding, Cornelius Driscoll lost his purse, which contained all of his savings. Under the circumstances, he thought it advisable to postpone his nuptials but after waiting for nearly a year, his intended bride lost patience with his constant dallying and sued him for breach of promise.

Catherine Mary Perry told the court that she had provided her own champagne silk and taffeta wedding dress, a going away outfit and all the bedroom furniture for their marital home.

'Has your wedding dress come in useful since?' asked Mr Justice Horridge.

'I have dusted a few pictures with it' replied Miss Perry.

She was awarded £35 damages.

North London / Reading

After his wedding in 1934, Edward Travis Ganu of North London was planning to drive with his bride for a honeymoon in Minehead.

As was customary on such occasions, the rear of Ganu's car had been decorated with tin cans and just married notices and, when Ganu stopped to remove them, he somehow broke the car's lighting circuit.

He twice interrupted his journey to try and fix the lights but was unable to do so. He continued until Reading, where he was flagged down by a police constable and booked for driving a car without lights.

Later appearing before magistrates at Reading, the explained that he had stopped twice, adding that he thought that no human being could do more, especially since it was the first day of his married life and he was '...anxious to get on.'

Although the usual fine for such an offence was 10 shillings, magistrate Sir A. Griffith-Boscawen took a more lenient view and fined him only 5 shillings.

Walworth

Twenty-five-year-old William Godfrey Youngman had been courting Mary Wells Streeter for some time before he proposed marriage to her, suggesting a wedding date of 11th August 1860. He told his fiancée that he had a private income of around £200 a year and that he was intending to take a house in Brighton and keep her as a lady. Once they became engaged, their courtship continued largely by correspondence and William's letters swiftly began to show a preoccupation with insuring Miss Streeter's life. From her replies, it was obvious that his fiancée was not at all keen to have life assurance and Youngman grew ever more persuasive on the matter.

In one letter, he wrote *'I cannot think you would love me'* when Mary refused to let him purchase an insurance policy and in another he wrote *'For your own sake, dearest girl do has (sic) I say.'*

Miss Streeter eventually capitulated. The banns for the wedding were read at the church of St-Martin-in-the-Fields on 15th, 22nd and 29th July, and on 25th July, accompanied by his fiancée, Youngman took out a policy with Argus Insurance for £100, paying the first quarterly premium of £0 10s 2d. The company had specifically asked if the person to be insured had ever had a relative die of consumption and, Miss Streeter answered 'No', even though her sister had died from the disease just three months earlier.

On 30th July, Miss Streeter went to stay with Youngman, who lived with his parents and two younger brothers at 16 Manor Place, Walworth. The following morning, Youngman's father went out early, after which other people living in the house heard a cacophony of thumps and crashes coming from the family's rooms. When they went to investigate, they found Youngman covered in blood. He claimed that his mother had gone berserk and killed his fiancée and his two young brothers and, in self-defence, he had grappled the knife away from her and now believed he had probably killed her.

One of the tenants went to fetch a policeman and, when PC John Varney arrived, William greeted him in his nightshirt saying 'Oh, policeman, here is a sight. What shall I do?' Varney told William to get dressed.

At this point, William's father John Youngman arrived home to be faced with the bodies of his forty-six-year-old wife, Elizabeth, his sons Thomas Neale Youngman and Charles Rayson Youngman, aged eleven and seven respectively and William's fiancée. 'Where's William?' asked John and when William saw him, he insisted 'This is all mother's doings, father.'

Since William had admitted killing his mother in self-defence, he was arrested and charged with her wilful murder. Meanwhile, post-mortem examinations were carried out on the four victims, finding that all had been stabbed in the chest and their throats either cut, stabbed, or both. William continued to insist that his mother was responsible for all of the murders and that he had only killed her in self-defence when she tried to turn her knife on him. However, Elizabeth Youngman was suffering from cancer of the womb and, although the doctor who examined her body later described her as '...tolerably healthy and inclined to be stout', her husband believed that she was rather frail and weak. In addition, nobody could comprehend why, having managed to disarm his attacker, William then found it necessary to kill her. A short time after the murders, the life assurance policy on Mary Streeter was found in a locked chest at the foot of William's bed and this finally sealed his fate.

While William was in custody, a young woman from Staffordshire presented herself to the police, having read about the murders in the newspaper. She showed them a framed photograph and asked if this was William Youngman. When the police said that it was, she told them that she knew him as William Godfrey. According to the young woman, she and Godfrey had been engaged and he had written her similar letters to those he sent to Miss Streeter, urging her to let him take out assurance on her life. However, as the date for their wedding neared, Youngman committed a burglary and was sentenced to twelve months' hard labour. Although he had begged the girl to wait for him, by the time he came out of prison, she had broken off their engagement and moved away so that he couldn't find him.

Court at the Old Bailey (author's collection)

William Youngman was tried at the Old Bailey only for the murder of his fiancée. Before Mr Justice Williams, he continued to maintain his innocence, blaming his mother for the murders of Mary and his two younger brothers.

Although he described himself as a tailor, William's last position was as a footman to physician James Andrew Duncan. The doctor testified in court that he was very familiar with cases of cancer of the womb, such as allegedly suffered by Elizabeth Youngman and the fact that she had been described as '...tolerably healthy and inclined to be stout' suggested that the disease was in its early stages. Duncan claimed that it was an extremely painful condition, which in itself, might make Elizabeth particularly irritable. It was revealed that Elizabeth's mother had died in a lunatic asylum, something that, according to Duncan, may have made her daughter more susceptible to homicidal mania, as could taking an opium-based medicine for pain relief.

Youngman's defence counsel, Mr Best, cross examined the medical witnesses, establishing that Elizabeth Youngman was, in their opinion, physically strong enough to have committed the murders of her sons and future daughter-in-law. Best argued that it was preposterous to imagine that his client should commit four brutal murders just for the sake of gaining £100 from an insurance policy. Dealing with the incriminating insurance, Best maintained that Youngman was actually being rather sensible in taking it out, given that his fiancée's sister had so recently died of tuberculosis.

Best made much of the history of insanity in Youngman's family, telling the court that not only had his maternal grandmother died insane, but also an uncle on his father's side of the family. Furthermore, Youngman's paternal grandfather had also spent time in an asylum.

The jury believed the prosecution rather than the defence and found William Godfrey Youngman guilty of wilful murder. He was sentenced to death, still protesting his innocence and taken to Horsemonger Gaol to await his execution. Before his death, he was visited by his father, brother and two sisters and promptly began berating John Youngman for being such a bad father to him and his siblings. The argument became so heated that John was taken to another room, to allow things to calm down.

Executioner William Calcraft (author's collection)

William Youngman approached his death with the same nonchalance that he had exhibited throughout his trial. Urged by the prison chaplain not to leave this world with a lie in his mouth, Youngman replied 'Well, if I wanted to tell a lie, it would be to say that I did it.'

On 4th September 1860, the morning of his execution, William breakfasted on bread, butter and cocoa, asking when he finished eating if he might have some more. A crowd of almost 20,000 people assembled outside the gaol to watch the execution and it was reported that those living in houses overlooking the gallows were charging spectators 1d each to watch from their upstairs windows.

When executioner William Calcraft led Youngman to the gallows, the condemned man instructed him to 'strap my legs tight and be sure to shake hands with me before I go.' Calcraft obliged on both requests.

Waterloo Station

Charles William 'Eric' Fogg was employed by the B.B.C. as a music director on the Empire Service (later the World Service). The thirty-six-year-old composer, conductor and musician was also known to thousands of children as 'Uncle Eric', having presented the radio programme 'Children's Favourites'.

On the night of 18th December 1939, Fogg stayed overnight in London with his friend Cedric Cliffe. The following morning, he left Cliffe's house in a taxi, intending to take his luggage to Waterloo Station, before lunching at Kenton and then keeping a business appointment. After that, he planned to travel by train to Bournemouth, where he was due to marry his second wife on 22nd December.

Shortly before midday, Fogg was standing on the platform at Waterloo Station when he suddenly either jumped or fell in front of a train and was fatally injured. The train driver later stated at the inquest that he had not actually seen Fogg leave the platform but had just seen him appear in front of his train, his hands outstretched as if he were diving.

The only witness to have actually seen what happened was a schoolboy named Claude Hoskins, who told coroner Mr F.H. Sewell that Fogg was '…walking about a bit' and then saw the train and fell over. Sewell asked the boy if he thought Fogg had fallen deliberately, to which Claude replied 'Yes, but he did not jump.'

Sewell tried to elicit more facts from Claude, who explained that Fogg had not been bent but was stiff when he fell. 'He might have felt giddy or faint but he did not jump' stressed the boy.

Nobody who knew Fogg had ever known him to suffer from fainting or dizzy spells and nobody could think of any reason why he might have killed himself. Eventually, the coroner summarised his findings, saying 'Having heard the evidence, I feel there is some doubt as to how this accident happened.' The inquest jury returned an open verdict.

Clapham Common

William Charles Phelps of Clapham had given his blessing to an engagement between his daughter, Flora Kate and thirty-four-year-old John Wellock Preston, a former Captain in the Tank Corps and now a commercial traveller. However, Phelps and the rest of Flora's family were completely unaware that the couple had secretly married on 31st May 1924, Flora returning home after the ceremony and her new husband remaining at his lodgings.

Flora and John went on holiday together between 5th and 13th September and, on their return, they finally broke the news of their marriage to her parents, who were both hurt and angry at being deceived.

On 15th September, one of Flora's brothers saw John outside their parents' house in Lydon Road and asked him what he was doing there. John said that he had come to say goodbye before shooting himself, at which the brother told him to 'Clear off' and went indoors. Almost immediately, he heard a gunshot and, looking out of the window, he saw his brother-in-law fall to the ground.

The shooting was witnessed by several other people, among them a little boy, who ran screaming to his mother and also a doctor who lived on Lydon Road. Dr Whitelaw hurried to the casualty but there was nothing he could do as Preston lay dying from a single gunshot to the head. His Army service revolver lay nearby, five of the six chambers still loaded. A note to his wife was found in his pocket, reading: '*I was blind and only madly in love with you as I shall be right up to the end and after. I must give in my cheques and go.*'

At the inquest on his death, his distraught widow told the coroner that her husband had suffered badly from malaria and insomnia and that he had previously threatened suicide. 'I think he thought it would make me happier if he were out of the way' she sobbed.

The inquest jury returned a verdict of 'suicide while of unsound mind', the coroner describing Preston's death as '... a self-sacrificing attempt to restore peace and happiness.'

Hampton

In December 1937, on the evening before his marriage to Priscilla White was due to take place, Teddington canvasser Arthur Edward Wyath took a last load of furniture to the house in Hampton where the couple planned to make their home. Unfortunately, his hand barrow was in collision with a trolley bus, and he sustained fatal injuries in the accident.

Tragically, Miss White attended her forty-nine-year-old fiancé's funeral on what should have been the couple's first full day of married life.

Kensington

On Saturday 8th March 1902, Miss Emily Daly married Frederick Allen. After the ceremony, the wedding party returned to the bride's parents' house at 12 Pembroke Square, Kensington, where a wedding breakfast had been prepared. When the bride and groom left for their honeymoon in Bedford, a number of wedding guests rushed out onto a balcony to shower them with rice and confetti as they drove away.

The balcony collapsed, throwing nine women and a child onto the street below. All were taken to West London Hospital, where eight were treated for minor cuts and bruises and discharged. The bride's grandmother, seventy-four-year-old Lydia Priesthill and another guest, thirty-four-year-old Annie Hall, were detained in hospital, Mrs Priesthill with a broken leg and Mrs Hall with cuts to her head.

Perhaps the luckiest of all was a lady named Mrs Mears, who fell onto railings beneath the balcony. The iron spikes missed her body completely, piercing only her clothing and leaving her dangling suspended in mid-air until she was rescued.

Pimlico

After his wedding at St Gabriel's Church, Pimlico, on 4th August 1907, Albert Jordan went for a walk with the best man and one of his bride's sisters, leaving his new wife Emily at their rented home with another sister, preparing the wedding breakfast. Albert was absent for about an hour and three quarters, when he returned home to find himself on the verge of becoming a widower.

Twenty-six-year-old Emily had been making custard on a methylated spirit stove when the flames caught her cream muslin wedding dress. Her sister, who had been dozing on a sofa, awoke to Emily's frantic screams and tried to beat out the flames with her bare hands. When her own clothes caught fire, she rushed out into the street shouting desperately for help.

Neighbour Henry Bungay rushed into the house and saw a woman enveloped in flames, '...one long blaze from the feet to the head'. Bungay tried to extinguish the fire by wrapping Emily in a coat and then a mat but the flames came through, at which he frantically tore off her clothes and stamped on them.

Firemen arrived to find Emily burned all over her body but conscious and she was rushed to hospital, along with her sister, who suffered severe burns to her arms and hands. Emily survived long enough to explain to Albert that she turned away from the methylated spirit stove to attend to some vegetables that were cooking on the fire and that her wedding dress had caught the spirit stove.

An inquest held by Coroner Mr Troutbeck at Westminster subsequently returned a verdict of 'accidental death.'

Barnet

In 1888, William Devon (76) and Caroline Lenman (71) applied to the Barnet Board of Guardians for continuation of the parish relief they had been receiving for some time. The couple had been living together for many years but had never married and Reverend G. Henesy objected to the couple being allowed any payment at all, given that they were 'living in sin.'

Since the couple were destitute, it was suggested that their benefits could continue if they were legally married. Guardian Mr Parsloe offered the use of his carriage, to convey the couple to and from church. Another Guardian, Dr Schmidt, offered to supply a smart coat for the bridegroom, while a third, Mr Simons, offered to contribute for a wedding cake.

The ceremony was going well, until the time arrived for Devon to put the ring on his bride's finger. The couple stared at each other blankly, since neither had realised the necessity of providing a ring. The ever-practical Mr Parsloe, who had given the bride away, suggested borrowing one from an elderly female who had acted as a bridesmaid. The ceremony was concluded and the newlyweds were driven home in Parsloe's carriage, a large crowd cheering them on their way.

Westminster

Thirty-year-old Major Howard Phillips Skinner M.B.E. was due to marry Miss Edna Honor Lawson on 3rd October.

Skinner arrived in London a couple of days before the wedding and stayed at The Norfolk Hotel on Surrey Street with his best man and some of his friends. On the day before the wedding, his mother joined the party from her home in Scotland. They had dinner together that evening and then retired to their separate bedrooms and, at some time during the night, Skinner apparently fell out of his bedroom window and was fatally injured.

At the inquest on his death, everyone in his party testified that he had been perfectly sober and very happy on retiring to bed. A letter he had written to his father only the day before was produced, in which he said how thrilled he was to be getting married and how much he was looking forward to being a husband.

Skinner's bed had been slept in and there was no sign of any disturbance in his hotel room. The coroner adjourned the inquest so that he might go and see the room himself.

When the proceedings resumed. Skinner's father suggested that he may have been sleepwalking. Apparently, he had frequently done so while at Preparatory School but his father was under the impression that he had grown out of the habit. However, it was highly possible that the stress and excitement of his imminent wedding may have caused him to sleepwalk again. The inquest jury returned a verdict of 'accidental death'.

The Norfolk Hotel (author's collection)

Maida Vale

On 23rd September 1926, the morning of his wedding to pharmacist Miss Elizabeth 'Betty' Will, twenty-eight-year-old Eric Stanley Chappell went with his brother, Kenneth, to visit his flat in Maida Vale, where building work was being undertaken. Chappell, himself a Master Builder, wanted to assure himself that the work was progressing satisfactorily and that the flat would be ready for him and his new bride on their return from honeymoon.

Chappell went to the third floor of the building to inspect the work being done by some electricians. From there, he seemed to vanish into thin air and it was some time before he was found impaled on the railings that separated his house from the one next door. Because the railings were in an inaccessible position, the fire brigade struggled to free him and, although he was rushed straight to hospital, he was found to be dead on arrival. A post mortem examination showed that he had six broken ribs, a torn heart and a punctured lung.

A window on the third floor of the property was found open, from which Chappell had apparently fallen. It was uncertain whether he had simply overbalanced while looking out of the window or whether he had deliberately climbed out, possibly to fix some wireless apparatus, and missed his footing. Nobody either inside or outside the house saw him fall. The one thing that was immediately ruled out was suicide, since Chappell had spoken to a neighbour only minutes before entering the house and appeared to be in the highest of spirits, laughing and joking about weddings generally and his own in particular. He and Betty had been engaged for three years and had ironically been forced to postpone their wedding from the previous year due to unavoidable and unforeseen circumstances.

The news of her fiancé's death was broken to the distraught bride as she was about to leave for All Soul's Church, London Road, where the ceremony should have taken place at two o'clock. Most of the guests were already at the Church when they were told that there had been an accident and that the wedding had been cancelled.

An inquest later returned a verdict of 'accidental death' on Mr Chappell. Shortly before his death, Chappell had withdrawn £700 from the bank and, although his wallet was never found, the coroner suggested that its weight may have caused him to overbalance.

Camberwell

On 24th December 1937- the morning of his wedding to Ida Rose Hall – twenty-three-year-old Edward Emblem arrived at his sister's house and asked her if he could borrow some money.

Emblem's sister's husband was about to go into hospital and she would soon be without his wage, so she told her brother that she had no money to lend him. Emblem was terribly upset. He began to cry and told his sister that if she couldn't let him have some money, he couldn't go through with the wedding.

When Emblem failed to appear at the church, his family went to the flat that was to be his new marital home. Finding the door locked and smelling gas, they called the police and when the door was broken down, Emblem was found dead, with his head in the gas oven. He was surrounded by wedding presents and was wearing the suit he had bought to get married in.

Everyone was shocked at the state of the flat. There was no marital bed, and no mattress, just sheets and a blanket arranged on the floor. Cardboard boxes and an old suitcase had been made into a table and the floors were covered in brown paper rather than linoleum.

When the police sergeant gave evidence at the inquest, Ida Hall almost collapsed when he described the condition of the flat and his sister fainted. When Ida was able to face giving evidence, she told the coroner that she and Edward had gone to prepare the flat on 23rd

December and there had been an argument about money. 'I was still willing to get married' she assured the coroner.

Edward had left two letters, one to Ida and a second to his mother, which read in part; *'My dear mother, I am sorry I had to do this. Please don't blame Ida. She had nothing to do with it.'*

The inquest found a verdict of 'suicide while the balance of his mind was disturbed when suffering from mental depression.'

St. Giles

On 7th October 1909, thirty-nine-year-old William English Carson arrived at the Registry Office in St Giles to marry Margaret Ann Davies. Registrar Mr Appleton noticed that Carson seemed to be in a very bad mood and he was so brusque and rude to his bride that Appleton took her aside before the ceremony.

Appleton asked Miss Davies if she thought that Carson was unwell and she replied that he was. He then asked her if she thought Carson was capable of going through with the ceremony. 'Oh, yes, he's quite able. He is doing this on purpose' Miss Davies assured him.

The registrar was so concerned by Carson's attitude and demeanour that he asked Miss Davies if this was what she really wanted, advising her to talk to her friends and think about what she was doing. The bride was not to be deterred and, with tears in her eyes, implored Appleton to go on with the ceremony.

Appleton turned his attention to Carson. 'Do you know why you are here?' he asked him.

'Yes, to marry this lady' answered the groom.

'Do you want to marry her?' asked Appleton.

'No, but if she insists, I have no objection' said Carson.

With Miss Davies begging him to go ahead, Appleton eventually began the ceremony. When it came to putting a ring on the bride's finger, Carson roughly thrust it on, then immediately tried to snatch it back but was thwarted by his bride. He refused to give his father's name and signed the register 'John Jones.' As soon as the wedding was over, he turned to his new wife and said 'There. I don't give a damn. I'm off to America in the morning and you will never see my face again.'

Mr Appleton was so perturbed by the unusual wedding that he reported his concerns to the Chief Registrar, who in turn contacted the police. Carson was arrested at a boarding house that evening, where it was discovered that he had indeed booked a ticket to travel to America the following morning on board the *Lusitania.*

He was charged with having inserted a false entry in the register, an offence that would earn him a life sentence if he were convicted. He told Detective Sergeant Seggals 'I was incapable at the time. What do you think of it? I was like a man insane. I haven't the slightest recollection of it.'

Carson, who was described both as an American journalist and a publisher's agent, was brought before magistrates at Bow Street Police Court to answer the charges against him. Chief magistrate Mr Curtis Bennett ruled that it was blatantly obvious to all concerned that Carson was either drunk or ill at the Registry Office and, that being the case, the registrar should not have gone ahead with the wedding. Taking that fact into account, Bennet did not feel that he could send Carson for trial, finding him not guilty and discharging him from court.

The fate of Miss Davies is not recorded. Suffice to say that when Carson finally did board the *Lusitania* in January 1911 bound for New York, he sailed alone.

Harlesden

On 4th August 1934, thirty-year-old Sidney Rudge travelled from Cardiff to attend the wedding of his sister Ethel to Thomas D. Jackson. At the reception afterwards, in a flat at Buchanan Gardens, there was a ready supply of whisky, port wine and beer and the guests all drank liberally as they enjoyed dancing and a sing-song.

Eventually, Sidney and his brother Clifford Henry Rudge both fell asleep, Clifford in an armchair and Sidney on the sofa. Clifford was later awakened by a man shaking him by the shoulder and, as he opened his eyes, he saw a man punch his brother Sidney in the face.

Sidney immediately fell to the floor unconscious and subsequently died.

At an inquest on his death, coroner Dr J. Crone asked if Clifford could identify the man who punched his brother and Clifford promptly pointed to Henry French.

Another wedding guest, Frank Ash, stated that French had tried to awaken both of the Rudge brothers to tell them that it was time to leave. Both men became antagonistic, demanding to be left alone to sleep. There was a brief struggle between French and Sidney Rudge, during which they both fell and crashed into a china cabinet, which shattered beneath them.

'How many people there were merry and bright' asked a juror at the inquest.

'Most of them' was the reply.

Importantly, Ash told the inquest that he had seen no blows exchanged between French and Sidney Rudge.

When French gave evidence, he admitted to having drunk two glasses of beer and three of whisky, saying that his memory was consequently a little hazy. He insisted that he had no grudge against either of the Rudge brothers and had never even met them before – he just woke them to tell them that it was time to go home and

Sidney promptly attacked him. French too denied that any blows had been struck.

A doctor certified that Sidney Rudge's death was caused by cerebral haemorrhage, caused by excessive drink and excitement. Having performed a post mortem examination, he had found no evidence of any injury to Rudge's skull nor of any blows.

The inquest jury returned a verdict of 'death by misadventure' but asked the coroner to caution French to control his temper, adding that, had he kept control of himself, the incident would in all probability not have occurred. French was not prosecuted for his part in Rudge's death.

Camberwell

The wedding of Major Henry Joseph Elcomb and Elizabeth Mary Smith was scheduled to take place at Camberwell Registry Office on 19th February 1944 and, on the eve of the wedding, the Elcomb family gathered at the bridegroom's parents' flat, ready to attend the ceremony the next day.

Tragically, a bomb fell on the flat that evening and the bridegroom and most of his relatives were killed. Major Elcomb's mother and sister perished, along with another sister, Marie Mitchell, her husband Clarence and their nine-month-old baby, Michael. Having travelled from Scotland for the wedding, the bride's brother, Albert, was also killed with his wife Dorothy and their five-month-old daughter, Carol Ann. Of the ten people in the flat when the bomb fell, only the bridegroom's father survived.

The bride was an orphan, who lived with her disabled sister in their aunt's home. She later said of her fiancé 'Now he is gone and there will never be another like him'.

Battersea

On 19th December 1906, twenty-three-year-old Frank Chambers (a.k.a. Harwood) took part in a boxing tournament at Battersea.

Considerably taller than his opponent, Albert Wilmot, Chambers fought the first two rounds vigorously. However, at the beginning of the third round, he suddenly began to stagger, looking dazed and rather confused. The referee signalled Wilmot to stop fighting and raised his arm in the air, proclaiming him the winner. Chambers was helped to his corner, then to his dressing room, where he almost immediately collapsed. A doctor was on hand and finding Frank in a comatose state, with a very feeble pulse, he ordered his removal to Bolingbroke Hospital.

Chambers died soon after admission and a post-mortem examination showed a large blood clot on his brain, probably due to the laceration of a blood vessel after a blow. There were no external bruises or even red marks on his face, head or chest but it was found that his skull was a little thinner on one side than the other.

Coroner Mr Troutbeck held an inquest on 23rd December at which Thomas Benjamin Chambers testified that his brother had been a healthy, strong and very fit man, who had only recently left the Army.

The fight had been watched by policeman Sub-Divisional Inspector Hodges, who told the inquest that it had been fought very fairly and that Wilmot had shown no signs of temper.

The coroner concluded that the contest had been properly conducted and that the organisers had done everything in their power to take the greatest care to ensure that it was safe. There was an element of risk in every sport and the only possible suggestion that the coroner could make was that perhaps the contestants might have been medically examined and pronounced fit before their fights. However, he acknowledged that, in this case, Chambers would undoubtedly have been given the green light to compete, since he was such a fit young man.

The inquest jury returned a verdict of 'accidental death' on Frank Chambers, who was to have been married on Christmas Eve.

Willesden

In June 1925, Mr A.C. Doran J.P., the chairman of Willesden Council, announced that he was setting up a fund to benefit George Wood and his fiancée Miss Sybil Fountain.

The couple had been engaged for five years, during which time they saved every spare penny for their future married life. In the run up to their wedding, they had withdrawn their life savings of £300. They had furnished their new marital home and paid for their wedding but two days before it was due to take place, their house burned down. All of the furniture was destroyed, along with the wedding dress and all of the bride's jewellery – even their remaining money was consumed by the fire – and sadly, nothing was insured.

The only thing that survived the inferno was the two gold wedding rings they had bought. Although the boxes were badly damaged, the two rings were as good as new. The bride and groom saw this as a good omen and decided to go ahead with their wedding, although as soon as the ceremony ended, instead of their anticipated honeymoon, Sybil went home to her mother and George went back to work to start saving all over again.

Barking

On 7th July 1910, thirty-seven-year-old compositor William James Harman married milliner Hildegard Clarice Gronland at the Roman Catholic Church in Barking. The couple had met in 1908 and had been engaged since Easter 1909. On the day after their wedding, they were planning to sail to South Africa, where Harman had secured a position with the *Cape Times*.

The newlyweds were enjoying their wedding reception with their guests, when a strange woman barged in and claimed to be Harman's wife. Since Louisa Mary Harman (nee Guire) had a copy of their marriage certificate, Harman could hardly deny it and admitted to his tearful bride of just three hours that he was already married.

Harman was brought before magistrates at Stratford charged with bigamy. It was revealed that he had been married to his first wife for seventeen years and they had four children together. He had continued to live at home, apparently happily, until the very day of his bigamous marriage. Having obtained a job in South Africa, the newspaper had paid for his berth aboard the *Grantully Castle*, also making him an allowance of seven guineas towards his wife's passage. Harman had fully intended to take his new bride and, if it wasn't for the fact that his first wife had spotted that he had taken his bags from their house and traced them to Barking, he might well have got away with it.

Before the magistrates, Miss Gronland sobbed bitterly, telling the court 'I don't want to prosecute. I don't want anything done to him at all.' In spite of her protests, the case was sent for trial at The Old Bailey.

Although Harman pleaded guilty in court, he made allegations of drunkenness and immorality against his first wife in the hope of a more lenient sentence. He was sentenced to twelve months' hard labour, which he served at H.M.P. Wormwood Scrubs. Hildegard went on to marry a man named Albert Smith in 1911.

Eastern

Market Deeping, Lincolnshire

September 1922 should have been a time for great celebration for the licensee of The White Horse Inn at Market Deeping, widow Mrs Edith Caroline D'Arcy. On 20th September Mrs D'Arcy's daughter Ivy Dora D'Arcy was married to her fiancé, hairdresser George Robert Prentice and instead of going on honeymoon, the young couple went home after their wedding in order to help Mrs D'Arcy prepare for her own wedding on 25th September.

On 23rd September, the new Mrs Prentice, her sister Gertrude and Eva (or Evelyn) Kitchener, who was soon to become Mrs D'Arcy's stepdaughter, were in the hall of the pub looking at wedding presents, which had been laid out on a table there.

Suddenly there was a loud bang and a shout and Ivy Prentice fell to the floor. The candle that the women had been using to look at the presents blew out but there was sufficient light for Mrs D'Arcy to see a man standing in the hall, pointing a shotgun straight at her. With great courage, Mrs D'Arcy charged at the man and managed to deflect his next shot, which went through a window and out into the street.

People came running from all directions and, when light was restored, it revealed Ivy lying on the floor, the front of her dress soaked with blood and a huge blood clot on her lap. The shooter was quickly identified as pub regular Frank Fowler, who looked dispassionately at Ivy, who he had known since her childhood and remarked 'I have had my revenge'.

A doctor was sent for but although Dr Benson arrived within minutes, he was too late to save Ivy who had died from shock and haemorrhage, a 2½ x 3inch wound on her left breast. Fowler was arrested and went quietly with the arresting officers.

The inquest was held on 25th September and before attending the proceedings, Mrs D'Arcy and her fiancé William James Owen Kitchener married quietly, having cancelled their reception and honeymoon. When the gun that Fowler had used was brought into court, Mrs D'Arcy sobbed 'That's the gun that shot my darling'. Describing Ivy as '...the brightest little thing that you could meet', she explained that Fowler had always had an unrequited love for Ivy and had consequently been very jealous of her relationship with George and had vowed to have his revenge on him. Ivy had never given him even the slightest encouragement, as he was almost twice her age.

The inquest jury returned a verdict of wilful murder against Fowler, who subsequently stood trial before Mr Justice Lush at the Lincolnshire Assizes. Counsel for the defence tried to show that Fowler was insane, calling his aunt Mrs Ann Orsman as a witness. Mrs Orsman employed her nephew as a farm labourer and told the court that, following his discharge from the army, his behaviour had been somewhat strange. He would curse and swear and then sing hymns. He complained of pains in his head and would frequently get up at night, thinking that people were looking at him through the windows. On one occasion he had threatened her with a knife and he had also shot her cat.

The defence also tried to show that Fowler's father was insane and that any son of his was likely to have similar traits. The prosecution produced medical evidence to counter this claim, convincing the jury that while Fowler's father was 'simple' and 'below average', he had never displayed symptoms of insanity or mental deficiency.

The jury found Fowler guilty as charged and he was sentenced to death. His sentence was appealed on the grounds of his possible insanity not being adequately communicated to the jury but the appeal was denied.

Thirty-five-year-old Fowler was hanged on Wednesday 13th December 1922 by Thomas Pierrepoint at Lincoln Prison, as part of a double execution with George Robinson, who had cut his former girlfriend's throat.

Newmarket, Cambridgeshire

A wedding took place at Newmarket on 5th February 1869, at which one of the guests was James Kennelly aged about eighteen years old. At the reception, Kennelly was one of a number of young men enjoying a game of cards, which included the groom's brother, William Allen, who sat next to him. All of a sudden, Kennelly stopped playing and toppled from his seat onto the floor, where he lay without moving.

Surgeon E. Donaldson arrived within half an hour to treat him, finding Kennelly very red in the face, his breathing slow and laboured. Donaldson prised open his mouth and found a huge lump of partially chewed meat and potatoes lodged in his throat. The surgeon managed to remove them and Kennelly immediately began to breathe more easily but a couple of hours later, the wedding party summoned the doctor again when Kennelly's breathing worsened.

Now Donaldson found Kennelly's jaw locked by a muscular spasm. He managed to prize his mouth open, inserting a knife handle between his teeth to prevent his jaw snapping shut. This time, Donaldson found that a collection of fluid had amassed in Kennelly's throat and, unable to cough it up, he was slowly suffocating. Donaldson managed to drain the fluid and, once again, Kennelly's breathing improved. The surgeon stayed with him for about an hour but almost immediately after he left, Kennelly expired.

Coroner Mr C.J. Daly held an inquest at which Donaldson attributed the cause of death to a quantity of mucus collecting on his chest, which he was unable to discharge.

Spilsby, Lincolnshire

Just before eleven o'clock on 2nd December 1939, police raided the Register Office at Spilsby and arrested the bridegroom only a few minutes before his wedding was due to take place. Forty-year-old

Harry Lilley had been on the verge of marrying eighteen-year-old Gwendoline Christina Robinson before the police were tipped off by the Registrar that Lilley had repeatedly represented himself as a bachelor, despite having another wife.

It emerged that Lilley had first married on November 18th 1918 but had separated from his wife in 1930. The couple, who had produced three children, briefly reunited before separating again in 1931.

Lilley had met Gwendoline in 1939 and told her that he was divorced. When he gave notice to the registrar of his intention to marry, he represented himself as a bachelor on the official documents and, when asked by the registrar shortly before the ceremony was due to take place, he continued to insist that this was correct.

Brought before Mr Justice Oliver at Lincolnshire Assises, charged with making a false declaration for the purpose of marrying, Lilley pleaded guilty. In his defence, he told the judge that he had believed that once he and his wife had been separated for seven years, he was automatically free to remarry.

Mr Justice Oliver commented that however ignorant Lilley might be, he knew that, having been married before, he could never be a bachelor. 'It is not the relationship between you and your wife that matters' Mr Justice Oliver told Lilley.' It is the fact that by means of this perjury, you were endeavouring to obtain possession of a young girl of eighteen and, indeed, were within a few minutes of doing so.'

Sentencing Lilley to six months' imprisonment, the judge told him that, had the wedding ceremony to Miss Robinson actually gone ahead, the sentence would have been considerably longer.

Wrestlingham, Bedfordshire

On 4th October 1881, seventy-seven-year-old Thomas Waldock married eighty-one-year-old Mary Minx. Both had been married twice before – both of Thomas's previous wives were called Mary and both of Mary's previous husbands were called Thomas.

Orby, Lincolnshire

After their wedding on 27th November 1811, Thomas Paul and his bride Sarah (nee Waite) and their guests went to dine with Mr Paul's parents at Orby.

For the wedding breakfast, Mrs Paul had prepared a roast goose, which she had stuffed with two whole penny loaves and two ounces of black pepper. Unfortunately, what she believed was black pepper was actually gun powder.

As the guests sat round the fire waiting for the goose to be cooked, Mrs Paul used a poker to stir the flames. As she did, a spark ignited the stuffing and there was a deafening bang as the goose exploded, showering the guests with fragments of meat and hot fat.

Fortunately, nobody was seriously injured, although the ladies' dresses were ruined by flying grease and the cooked goose was missing from the wedding feast.

Cambridge, Cambridgeshire

It was reported in 1876 that a marriage had been solemnised at the Cambridge Registry Office between Robert George Jackson and the daughter of the vicar of a neighbouring parish. Jackson, who was nineteen years old, was employed as a coprolite digger and was both illiterate and lame. In contrast, his bride was said to be most accomplished, speaking seven or eight languages fluently.

It was reported in the contemporary newspapers that Jackson was so illiterate that he was '...deficient of the commonest rudiments of education and by no means makes up this lack by personal attractions.'

Aldborough, Norfolk

Aldborough Hall (author's collection)

On 2nd April 1931 – her twenty-sixth birthday – domestic servant Kathleen Borrett went to collect her fiancé Alma John Strong from Aldborough hall, where he worked as an under gamekeeper. The couple should have been going to Aldborough Church, where they were due to marry that morning – instead they were found lying in a field by estate steward Abraham Newstead, a double-barrelled shotgun nearby. Kathleen was dead from gunshot wounds and her fiancé was mortally wounded and would die in hospital later that day.

At an inquest on their deaths, held on 4th April, Kathleen's grandfather John Borrett told the enquiry that he had not approved of the marriage, as he didn't like Strong's disposition. He had told his granddaughter that, as far as he was concerned, she would be better off buried than married to Strong.

Strong's father had also been against the marriage, although he had merely advised his son to postpone the wedding until he got more permanent employment. He revealed that his son had been wounded no less than eight times during the War, one of the injuries being to his head, which caused him to suffer from depression.

Although Kathleen and Alma had met years previously, Kathleen had then moved away from the area and the couple had only been courting for a couple of months before the banns were read for their wedding. People who knew thirty-six-year-old Strong expressed surprise at the speed with which his courtship progressed.

Although the coroner returned a verdict that Strong shot Kathleen and then shot himself, they found no evidence as to the state of his mind at the time. Furthermore, nobody was able to give a satisfactory explanation for the blood that was found in the lane leading up to the field where Kathleen lost her life.

Gedney, Lincolnshire

In 1892, it was reported that a woman had married in the Parish Church at Gedney wearing nothing but a sheet, which had been sewn up like a bag, leaving holes at the side for her bare arms. The bride, who walked barefoot to the altar, was a widow with four children, who was deeply in debt. It was widely believed that a man who married a woman dressed only in a sheet was acknowledging to the world that she brought nothing into the marriage and he would therefore not be personally liable for any of her previous debts.

Ipswich, Suffolk

On 22nd September 1937, on what should have been her wedding morning, cook Muriel Daisy Norton attended an inquest on the death of her fiancé, thirty-year-old butcher's assistant Maurice Charles Plumbly.

The couple were to have been married on 19th September but Plumbly told his fiancée that there was a problem at the Registry Office, which necessitated postponing the ceremony, so he had rearranged the wedding for 22nd September at St Peter's Church, Ipswich.

The couple had been together for three years and, according to Miss Norton, had never had a quarrel. They had rented and furnished a house together and she believed that both were looking forward to starting their married life.

On the morning of the wedding, Plumbly was found in a stable, shot between the eyes with a humane killer. When his distraught fiancée went to cancel the wedding arrangements, she found that none had been made.

Plumbly's brother told the inquest that he had been 'a bit moody' in the weeks leading up to the wedding but, apart from that, nobody had seen any signs whatsoever that he intended to take his own life. The inquest recorded a verdict of 'suicide while the balance of his mind was disturbed.'

Yarmouth, Norfolk

On 14th May 1909, Robert Dennington married Annie French at Yarmouth. As the happy couple left the church, the bridegroom's aunt, Mrs Edith Hindes, stepped forward and snatched at the bride's veil, tearing a hole in it. She then proceeded to '...assail the bride with language of the vilest description, containing equally vile accusations.' Two days after the wedding, Mrs Hindes approached her nephew 'like a tigress' with a pick axe in her hands, pushed him and further insulted his wife.

Dennington took his aunt to Yarmouth Police Court, assuring magistrates there that this wasn't done with any intention of being vindictive but because he was afraid that 'mud sticks' and numerous people had heard the entirely unfounded accusations made against his new wife, the only one of which that the contemporary newspapers dared to print was that she was 'a good-for-nothing hussy'.

Mrs Hindes flatly denied having made any such accusations. She swore that the bride's veil had simply become caught on her coat as she walked past and it had torn as she had tried to untangle it. However, numerous witnesses contradicted her statement and magistrates found the case against her proven. She was fined twenty shillings plus costs, with one month's imprisonment if she could not pay and Dennington was told to return to court should she cause him or his wife any further trouble.

Skegness, Lincolnshire

On 24th November 1939, Ernest Cooper (19) and Frank Leslie Drury (23) appeared before magistrates in Skegness for the third time on a charge of robbery with violence.

Solicitor Mr. W. M. Attale of Lincoln appeared for Drury and as the court approached the lunchtime recess, he asked magistrates if Drury might be allowed bail during the lunch break or might be allowed to leave the court under supervision, since he was supposed to be getting married that afternoon at St Matthew's Church. The wedding was scheduled for 1.30 p.m. and Drury's fiancée was in court, with a special license and a wedding ring.

Attale told the Bench that the police had initially had no objections to the wedding going ahead but, since it was such an unusual request, officers had thought it prudent to clear it with the Chief Constable before granting permission. The Chief Constable had voiced strong objections but, according to Attale, the final decision rested with the Bench.

Magistrates decided that Drury's offence was too severe for him to be granted permission to marry.

He was later sentenced at the Lincolnshire Assizes to three years' penal servitude for his part in the robbery. Serving his time in the Borstal at Portland, the governor there later stated 'In my opinion, he is lower than any young man I have ever had through my hands, a persistent thief, cowardly, violent and vindictive.'

Godmanchester, Huntingdonshire

James Billings and Elizabeth Bates were married on 13th June 1880. Billings was exceptionally tall and his bride was very much shorter – in fact only a little shorter than the best man.

The vicar who performed the ceremony was a stranger to the parish and did not know any of the wedding party at all. It was only after the ceremony, when he saw the newlyweds walking off together that he realised that he had wrongly assumed that the best man was the bridegroom and had married the wrong couple.

When the bride and the man she assumed was her new husband got home, they were confronted by the Parish Clerk, who demanded that they return to the Church immediately. There the mix up was explained to them and with all parties having sworn an oath that the first ceremony had been performed in ignorance, the wedding was repeated, this time with Billings as the groom.

Immingham, Lincolnshire

Railway shunter William Stamp and Ethel Welton were married on 19 May 1914 and, three days later, they were at their marital home in Spring Street, Immingham, awaiting the delivery of their furniture.

William had told Ethel that he had saved up £60 and, as the wedding had cost £10, he had £50 left to pay for the furniture on delivery. When it arrived, he told Ethel to go upstairs to their bedroom and fetch his purse, containing his money. When she came downstairs to say that she couldn't find it, he immediately became upset, telling her 'I've been robbed!'

Ethel had never actually seen the £50 that William purported to have saved. 'You have not deceived me, have you Bill?' she asked him.

'You cannot trust me, can you?' replied her husband.

'Yes, I have always trusted you' she reassured him.

William went upstairs to look for his purse and when he didn't come down again, Edith went to look for him. She found him lying on their bedroom floor, his throat cut.

Ethel was so shocked that she screamed and ran out into the street, where her distress attracted the attention of two policemen. Sergeant Hessle and P.C. Bemrose went into the house with her, finding that William had somehow managed to lock the bedroom door. The policemen broke the door down but William bled to death before a doctor could be summoned. A notebook was found in front of him, in which he had started a suicide note, reading; *'Dear wife, just a last fare...'*

At the inquest on his death, the coroner said that he could only assume that William had deceived his wife about his savings and, when the furniture arrived and he couldn't pay for it, he was too ashamed to tell the truth. William's doctor stated that he had already been treated for scarlet fever and influenza that year, although he was uncertain if that would have any bearing on his death.

The inquest jury returned a verdict of 'suicide while of unsound mind.'

Note: The majority of the contemporary newspaper reports on the suicide give William's forename as Walter. Official records suggest that William is the correct name.

Yoxford, Suffolk

Yoxford (author's collection)

When gardener George Cady married Miss Sarah Jane Mason at Yoxford on 1st August 1898 - which was also his 30th birthday - he asked some of his fellow villagers to 'fire him a salute'. One of the men who did so was nineteen-year-old fisherman William Leverett.

The village innkeeper, Arthur James Doddington, lent his unloaded gun to a man named William Gilbert for the purpose of firing the salute. Gilbert loaded the weapon with gunpowder and brown paper and fired it in his front yard. At this, the new Mrs Cady came outside and asked them not to fire the gun so close to the house, as her mother-in-law was unwell. Gilbert again loaded the gun with powder and paper and gave it to William Leverett. The gun went off accidentally, so Gilbert loaded it a third time and watched Leverett walk away with it. A few minutes later, Leverett came back and told Gilbert 'I believe I have put the lamp out.'

Seconds later, cries of 'He's shot' rang out from the Cady's home, where their wedding breakfast was in full swing. The wedding party were assembled in a small room, with a ceiling that was only 6'4" high. Cady was a tall man and his head almost reached the ceiling. Seeing a lamp burning in the room, Leverett had decided to fire through the open window with the object of extinguishing it. He succeeded, but tragically a piece of wadding from the gun struck Cady's neck with tremendous force, ripping the flesh and exposing the carotid artery. Cady lingered in agony for eight days, before dying from tetanus.

On the day after the shooting, Leverett had gone to sea at Scarborough. However, when he received a telegram informing him of Cady's death, he immediately returned to Yoxford and handed himself in to the police. Unable to raise enough money for bail, he was held at Ipswich Gaol pending an appearance before magistrates.

Meanwhile coroner Mr C.W. Chaston held an inquest on Cady's death. It emerged that several young men had been 'skylarking' around Cady's home on the evening of his wedding. One person had fired a musket, leaving more than 40 shotgun pellets embedded in the back door. Leverett admitted to firing his gun through the open window, in order to extinguish the lamp, claiming that he had been somewhat drunk at the time and had not noticed the people in the room. The inquest found a verdict of manslaughter against him and he was committed for trial at the next assizes.

Appearing before Mr Justice Hawkins, Leverett pleaded guilty to manslaughter. His case was treated with a lot of sympathy, with even the prosecution agreeing that this was '...a foolish act, which ended in tragedy', with no animosity or malice whatsoever between the accused and the victim.

After hearing the facts, Hawkins announced that he intended to consider the case overnight and decide on an appropriate sentence. When the court reassembled the next day, Hawkins decried the custom of firing shots at weddings, saying that it was a practice that could be prosecuted under the Highways Act and should be stopped immediately.

Turning to Leverett, the judge said that he could not look to the sympathy shown towards him, nor to his prior reputation for good conduct and hard work. Rather, the judge intended to focus on the suffering that he had inflicted upon Sarah Jane Cady, who had devotedly nursed her husband until his death. The judge was also very much aware of the cruel mode of Cady's death, as a sole result of the defendant's reckless misconduct.

'The minimum sentence I could possibly award is one of nine months' hard labour', concluded Hawkins, adding that Leverett was merely being punished for his recklessness, which was visited by such fearful consequences. You have not forfeited any of your good character, Hawkins reassured Leverett.

In the wake of Cady's death, coroner Mr Chaston wrote to the *Eastern Daily Press,* appealing for donations for Sarah Jane Cady, an orphan who was left penniless by the tragedy and was at that time, too ill from shock and distress to return to domestic service.

West Midlands

Coventry, Warwickshire / Downham Market, Norfolk

On Wednesday 14th September 1938, William Eric Temple (29) and his fiancée Betty (or Bessy) Baldock attended a rehearsal at Coventry Cathedral, three days before their planned wedding. Said to be a very religious couple, they listened intently as Provost Very Reverend R.T. Howard explained the importance and sanctity of marriage. Shortly afterwards, Temple remarked anxiously to the Provost that he wasn't sure that he was worthy of 'the idealistic state of marriage' that had been depicted.

Immediately after the wedding rehearsal, Temple disappeared. Coventry City Police were informed that he was missing on 16th September, at which point his fiancée reluctantly postponed the wedding.

Temple was found at Downham Market in Norfolk, on what should have been the morning of his wedding. When farm labourer John Neave went to a cowshed, he noticed a pitchfork standing outside it, on which had been stuck a note reading. *'Fetch the police and don't look inside if you don't want to see a dead body'.* On opening the door, Neave found Temple hanging from a beam. He had obviously stood on an old oil drum to reach the beam, wrapped a rope around his neck and then kicked the oil drum away, leaving himself suspended. Letters to his family and fiancée were found in his pocket, along with a new gold wedding ring.

At the inquest, the coroner remarked that, from the content of the letters, it was obvious that Temple believed himself to be unworthy of his fiancée and, indeed, of marriage itself. He and Betty were said to be on the best of terms, having made all the preparations for their wedding and honeymoon and furnished a house in Coventry for their married life. Temple had a good, secure job as a draughtsman for the General Electric Company and had no money worries at all. However, he was said to be of rather a nervous disposition and suffered from anxiety.

The inquest returned a verdict that Temple died from 'asphyxiation caused by hanging himself while the balance of his mind was disturbed.'

Fenton, Staffordshire.

Twenty-one-year-old collier Samuel Flackett and twenty-two-year-old housekeeper Harriett Appleyard were married at Fenton on 13th October 1913. During the ceremony, Harriett complained of feeling a little faint and a chair was provided for her to sit down. She recovered sufficiently to walk the short distance home, where a wedding breakfast had been prepared to celebrate the occasion.

However, the food and drink remained untouched as, no sooner had she reached home, than she collapsed. A doctor was called to attend her but she died shortly before noon, leaving Samuel a bachelor, husband and widow within less than three hours. The doctor confirmed that the cause of her death had been 'too much excitement'.

Worcester / Dudley

On 24th June 1879, twenty-two-year-old Susan Little went to the Shire Hall, Worcester, to summon baker William Henry Ballard for bastardy. Ballard had never denied paternity of baby Francis, born in January 1879. However, he desperately wanted to marry Susan and refused to contribute towards the child until they were wed.

As Susan waited for her case to be heard, William approached her and asked how she was. 'Very well' replied Susan cordially.

William asked after Francis and Susan gave the same response.

William then asked to speak to Susan privately before they went into court but Susan's brother stepped between them and told William in no uncertain terms to go away. William complied but, moments later, Susan felt someone come up behind her and before she could react, her throat had been cut.

Fortunately, a Dr Everett was attending court on a different matter and rushed to her aid. The cut was about 2½ long and quite superficial - no major blood vessels were severed. William, who had also tried unsuccessfully to cut his own throat, was promptly arrested and charged with attempted murder.

Mr Justice Hawkins (author's collection)

He appeared before Mr Justice Hawkins at the Worcester Assizes. The court was told that, at the time of the offence, Susan worked as a wet nurse for the family of Reverend William Berkeley at Cotheridge,

Worcestershire. After the birth of her own baby, Susan and Ballard fully intended to get married and set a date in February 1879 for the ceremony. Sadly, there was a problem with the bans and the wedding was rescheduled for 27th April. but Reverend Berkeley refused to allow Susan time off to get married, believing it would disrupt his own daughter's routine too severely. Susan pleaded with him, promising to come straight back to work after the ceremony and to stay on in her position as long as his infant daughter needed a wet nurse but Berkeley would not relent. Instead, he went into Worcester without consulting her and started affiliation proceedings against Ballard, only discussing the matter with Susan when he realised that he needed her signature on the documents.

With both Susan and William insisting that they wanted to marry, Mr Justice Hawkins made an unusual decision. When the jury found Ballard guilty of unlawful wounding, he deferred sentencing for a day, then called the couple back into court.

'You tell me that the prisoner behaved well to you up to the time this took place?' he asked Susan.

'Yes, my lord.'

'You have never had any real quarrel with him?

'No, my lord'.

'He always treated you with kindness?'

'Always, my lord.'

'Are you afraid of him?'

'No, my lord.'

Mr Justice Hawkins then addressed William, telling him that, in his opinion, the jury had been rather lenient in their verdict. The judge then discharged Ballard on a bond of £100, on the condition that he married Susan Little without delay. 'If you should behave badly towards her, you will be called up for judgement to receive that sentence that, under other circumstances, it would be my duty to pass' Hawkins warned Ballard.

Mr E. B. Evans, the High Sherriff of Worcestershire, arranged for a special licence and the couple were married at eight o'clock the next morning, at the church of St Mary Magdalene in Worcester, with Hawkins paying for the wedding ring out of his own pocket.

In an ideal world, they should have lived happily ever after. However, in 1880, thirty-six-year-old labourer Henry Salis was arrested in Dudley, charged with having deserted his wife and six children at Inkberrow, leaving them chargeable to the parish of Alcester. Salis was married to William Ballard's sister, Ellen, and, after stealing most of William's worldly goods, Susan had run away with her brother-in-law.

At some point before Salis's arrest, Susan tried to return to her husband but he refused to have anything to do with her. It is believed that she then spitefully informed the authorities of Salis's whereabouts. At the Alcester Petty Sessions, he was found guilty of desertion and sentenced to three month's hard labour.

The census of 1881, shows that Salis was subsequently reunited with his wife and children and the family were living with his father-in-law, George Ballard. Meanwhile, William Ballard was working and boarding at a baker's shop in Walsall, with little Francis. It has not proved possible to establish Susan's situation.

Wolvey, Warwickshire

On Christmas Eve 1919, thirty-seven-year-old Mrs Miriam (or Mariam) Garrett was attending her sister Ann Elizabeth 'Lizzie' Johnson's wedding at Wolvey Parish Church with her six children, when she suddenly slumped into the lap of a fellow guest, Marguerite Rolls.

As it was immediately obvious that she was quite dead and as the vicar was nearing the end of the ceremony, quick thinking guests surrounded her body and the service concluded without the happy couple being aware of the tragedy. An inquest later attributed her death to an attack of syncope, due to latent heart trouble, accelerated by the excitement of the wedding.

Peopleton, Worcestershire

On 30th December 1931, twenty-six-year-old Laura Perkins was making last-minute preparations for her wedding the following day when she began to feel unwell. She was rushed to Worcester Infirmary in a state of collapse and died in the early hours of the morning of what should have been her wedding day.

Until recently, Miss Perkins had worked as the second matron at King's Grammar School, Worcester, but she and her fiancé Frederick Birchley were due to start jobs as caretakers for a new school at Pershore after their wedding.

Miss Perkins was buried in her wedding dress, her bouquet and her bridesmaid's bouquet placed in her coffin, along with the wedding favours she should have received. The service was held at the same church where she should have celebrated her marriage.

Hanley, Staffordshire

The wedding between twenty-year-old Annie Tunnicliffe and Samuel Nixon had been arranged for 9th August 1905 and, on 5th August, Annie left her home in Hanley, saying that she was going to visit her fiancé. It was the last time that she was seen alive.

Soon afterwards, a note was found in her bedroom;' *Good-bye to all. I am better off the earth than on it. Mother and father don't worry after me. You will know the ending of me. There is none of my sisters that will give me a good name but hoping that they will all follow me to the cemetery. Don't worry after me. Give my best love to Sam and especially tell him not married on earth but married in heaven.'*

Given the content and tone of the letter, an immediate search was launched for Annie and the police began to drag nearby canals and ponds. She was eventually found drowned on what should have been the day of her wedding, in a notorious local spot on the Caldon Canal called 'Prime's Hole.' (This had been the site of a tragic double drowning of a courting couple just one month earlier and, by strange coincidence, a man named Steele found both Annie's body and the body of one of the previous victims, Louisa Whitehouse.)

At an inquest on Annie's death, the coroner expressed surprise that she had a large cut over her right eye and a compound fracture of her right arm, with the bone sticking out of her shoulder. Samuel Nixon was devastated by the loss of his fiancée and wanted to place his wedding ring on her finger before she was buried. However, the ring, which was in Annie's possession could not be found and, after taking evidence of identity, the coroner adjourned the inquest so that further investigations could be made.

When the inquest was resumed, it was revealed that Annie's father had been out of work and the Tunnicliffe family were struggling to survive. Sam had given Annie money to pay into a holiday club and this had disappeared, as had the wedding ring. In addition, some items of Sam's clothing had been pawned, apparently by Annie's mother.

The coroner suspected that Annie had either pawned or sold her wedding ring and used the money, along with the club money, to support her family and, with the wedding imminent, she could not bear to face the music when her actions were found out. The inquest returned a verdict of 'suicide while of unsound mind'. Annie was buried in her royal blue wedding dress and her sisters Tillie, Selina and Hannah did indeed follow her to the cemetery.

Oldberrow, Worcestershire

On 4th July 1963, a small wedding took place at Oldberrow Church in Worcestershire. There were only five people at the ceremony – the bride, the bridegroom, the vicar and the bride's mother and brother.

The vicar didn't seem too familiar with the wedding service, frequently stumbling over his words. And when the time came to sign the register, the bride's mother, Mrs Emily Martha Russell noticed that it was done in an ordinary lined exercise book rather than a more official document.

Mrs Russell was suspicious and asked to see a marriage certificate, which bridegroom Maurice John Else (33) assured her was coming in the post. However, alarm bells began to ring when the bride's brother mentioned to family friend Reverend Harold Sly that the vicar had not worn a surplice, Sly suspected that the wedding had been a fake and notified the police of his suspicions.

Else was questioned and found to be a married man from Dublin with four children. The 'vicar' who officiated at the wedding was his friend, Malcolm James Emery Kemp (44), who had hired his cassock and clerical collar from a theatrical costumier.

The bride was twenty-nine-year-old Lilian Mary Russell and she had absolutely no suspicions that she wasn't legally and properly married. It emerged that she was pregnant and when she had first suggested marriage to Else, he had told her that he was already married and was waiting for his divorce to come through. As her pregnancy progressed, Mary became ever more anxious that her child would be born outside wedlock and pressed Else to marry her as soon as possible.

Else suggested that the two of them should go to Plymouth for a few days, then come back and tell everyone that they had got married there. However, Mary refused to deceive her mother and so Else devised another plan. He told Kemp that he and Mary had married at Plymouth but that her mother was terribly upset to have missed the ceremony. Thinking he was doing a good turn, Kemp agreed to play the part of a clergyman so that the bride's mother could see her daughter getting married.

Kemp was subsequently charged with '...wilfully and knowingly solemnizing a marriage according to the rites of the Church of England by falsely pretending to be in Holy orders', while Else was charged with aiding and abetting him. After appearing before magistrates, both were sent for trial at the Assizes.

Mr Justice Elwes stated 'I do not punish you for seducing or deceiving that girl – those are moral offences of which the law doesn't take cognisance.' He then fined Kemp £50 and sentenced Else to nine months' imprisonment, while Mary Russell sobbed in court, saying 'I still love Maurice very much and I am praying that eventually we will be able to marry'.

Both men appealed their sentences and on 28th January 1964, their convictions were quashed by the Court of Appeal. It was decided that Mr Justice Elwes had misdirected the jury by failing to instruct them that, in order to convict, they had to be satisfied that Kemp had intended to deceive.' Obviously, when Kemp's appeal was successful, Else's conviction was also quashed, since he could not be found guilty of aiding and abetting an offence that had technically not happened.

Records show that Mary Russell and Maurice Else eventually married legally in 1965.

Hockley Heath, Solihull

After his wedding to thirty-one-year-old Miss Eileen Mary Hine on 15th June 1938, sixty-three-year-old businessman Clement John Newey began to feel unwell. A doctor was called but by six o'clock that evening, Newey had slipped into unconsciousness and he died shortly afterwards.

Newey and his new bride had planned a short honeymoon, after which they intended to travel abroad on business. Instead, the new Mrs Newey found herself returning home with her parents.

Tividale, Staffordshire

After their wedding on 21st December 1940, twenty-year-old Florence Lily Jones (nee Pottinger) and her husband Sidney James Jones were enjoying their reception at The Boat Inn, Tividale. The couple were standing by the piano leading a sing-song, when there was a tremendous crash and an anti-aircraft shell burst into the pub, landing in the cellar where it exploded. The injured, dead and dying were taken to Guest Hospital at Dudley.

Guest Hospital, Dudley (author's collection)

The bomb claimed thirteen victims, including the bride and her fifteen-year-old brother, David. The bridegroom's father lost his wife, son and brother, while the bridegroom was among numerous members of the wedding party who were seriously injured, losing a foot.

There was no ongoing air raid at the time and it was widely believed that the shell came from an accidental discharge of a Big Bertha gun, located at City Road, Tividale.

Note: Some sources state that the tragedy occurred on 23rd December 1940 rather than 21st December.

West Bromwich, Staffordshire

Everything was arranged for the marriage of twenty-year-old Sarah Anne Phillips to her fiancé Mr Scott on 20th June 1888. Yet, on the appointed day, Scott did not turn up to escort his bride to the church and she waited for him in vain as the hour at which the wedding was supposed to take place came and went.

Sarah begged her mother to come out with her to look for Scott but there was no trace of him, until somebody mentioned that he had left town that day. Sarah was distraught. She accompanied her mother home, then said she was going out for a walk and wanted to be alone.

While out walking, Sarah visited three different shops, buying a penny's worth of laudanum in each and, when she got home, she went into the front room and drank it all. When her mother found her with the empty bottles, Sarah was still conscious and kissed her mother, begging her forgiveness. She died in West Bromwich Hospital on what should have been her wedding night.

It is reported that Scott went to the hospital but was not allowed to see Sarah's body. He promised to attend the inquest and explain his conduct but didn't keep that appointment either.

The inquest jury heard that Scott was already married to another woman and that this was the second time that Sarah had been jilted by a man. Coroner Mr Hooper remarked that he found Scott's behaviour abominable and believed he should be horsewhipped. The inquest jury found a verdict of 'suicide while of unsound mind.'

Nuneaton, Warwickshire

Nuneaton Parish Church (author's collection)

In October 1919, having travelled from Birmingham, Sarah Ann Inns turned up at Nuneaton Parish Church late for her wedding to twenty-eight-year-old Walter Smith, only to be told that the wedding had already taken place and the newlyweds had left the church. When Sarah protested that the wedding couldn't have happened without her - the bride - Smith and his new wife were summoned back to the church to explain themselves.

Smith was a Romany Gypsy and, when his bride hadn't arrived at the church in time for the ceremony, he had asked her sister to deputise for her, believing that he could marry 'by proxy.' By coincidence, although they were sisters, both women were widows and had exactly the same name – Sarah Ann Inns. The now married

Sarah had four children, while the Sarah who should have been married had none.

Walter later made a statement, saying: 'I understand that according to an old Romany custom, marriage by proxy is allowed. I arranged with my sweetheart's sister to act in her stead. It was all done on the spur of the moment. I recognise my folly and am obtaining my solicitor's advice with a view to the abrogation of the ceremony.'

In the eyes of both the law and the church, the marriage between the two was legally binding and the newlyweds decided not to press for an annulment. The new Mrs Smith later told reporters:' The marriage was a mistake but now that it's taken place, we've decided to let it rest. It would take a great deal of money to undo what's been done and it seems the best thing we can do is stay married.'

Brades Village, Staffordshire

Twenty-one-year-old Lilian Wharton worked as a barmaid in her father's pub, The Fountain Inn at Brades Village. By 1913, she had been courting twenty-eight-year-old Thomas Fletcher for a year and their wedding was planned for 26th March that year.

The day before the wedding, Thomas went to visit Lilian at the pub and was taken aside by her mother, Mrs Eliza Jane Wharton. Mrs Wharton suggested to Thomas that he would be better off waiting until he could provide a proper home before rushing into marrying her daughter. Thomas suggested that the wedding could go ahead and Lilian could live with her parents until he had sorted out somewhere for them to live but Mrs Wharton still wasn't happy. She also told Thomas that she would much prefer it if he and Lilian had a church wedding, rather than marrying at Dudley Registry Office as they had planned.

Thomas had no choice but to agree with his future mother-in-law and the wedding was duly postponed.

However, Lilian did not seem to be in any hurry to set a new date and Thomas began to get the feeling that she and her family felt that he was not good enough for them. Having brooded over the matter for a few days, he visited a pawnbroker and bought a gun.

On 1st April 1913, he went to The Fountain Inn and ordered two glasses of brandy. He was served by Mrs Wharton, who then withdrew to allow Thomas and Lilian to talk. Moments later there was a loud bang and Mrs Wharton turned to see her daughter staggering towards her moaning 'Tom has shot me.' Lilian then turned and walked out into the street, where she collapsed.

Lilian had been shot in her left-hand side and doctors were unable to locate the bullet. On 8th April 1913, she died from peritonitis. Meanwhile, Thomas had shot himself in the face and, although he lost an eye, he survived to stand trial at the Worcester Assizes, where he pleaded 'not guilty' to the charge of the wilful murder of his fiancée.

Confident of being acquitted, he had already told the police:' I suppose I shall have to go through it for this when I get better. It don't matter (sic) they can't hang me. I have not killed her; it was her fault. I only fired two shots at her. I wish I had killed myself.'

In court, Thomas testified that he had bought the gun with the sole aim of committing suicide and had never had any intentions of hurting Lilian. When he pulled out the gun to shoot himself, Lilian tried to wrest it from his hand and it must have gone off accidentally.

The jury did not believe his story and found him guilty of wilful murder. As Mr Justice Bray pronounced the death sentence, both Thomas and his sister fainted from shock and several of the spectators in court became hysterical.

Thomas Fletcher was hanged on 9th July 1913 at Worcester Prison by John Ellis and his assistant Thomas Pierrepoint.

Hereford, Herefordshire

Miss Alice Tisdale met dairy farmer James Edward Sinnett in 1918. In February 1920, Sinnett promised to marry her, presenting her with an engagement ring in August of that year. By then, Alice had apparently allowed her fiancé 'certain liberties' and a wedding was quickly arranged for 7th December 1920.

On the 4th December, Alice and James arranged to meet in Hereford to make a few last-minute purchases for their wedding. James didn't turn up at the agreed time and Alice later found out by reading the local newspaper that he had actually sailed for Canada that morning.

Twenty-six-year-old Alice had played the organ at the local parish church for ten years and had received generous presents from parishioners and also the local village club in anticipation of her wedding. Now, she had the humiliating task of returning the gifts, not to mention the disgrace and shame of giving birth to an illegitimate child. (Her baby was born on 6th February 1921).

Alice sued Sinnett for breach of promise, telling the court that she had spent £75 of her own money in preparing for her marriage. Dismissing Sinnett's behaviour as '...cowardly, brutal and callous', the court awarded her £400 in damages.

Birmingham, Warwickshire

There was no love lost between Mr and Mrs Adams of Icknield Port Road, Birmingham, and their neighbour, steelwork erector Edward Bailey. Seventy-four-year-old Francis Adams and forty-nine-year-old widower Bailey had clashed numerous times before and were no longer on speaking terms.

On 29 May 1928, Bailey remarried and, as he was taking his new wife home after the ceremony, he met Adams at his garden gate. The two men got into an argument and, according to Mrs Adams, Bailey struck her husband on the chest. As Adams was walking up the garden path to his house he fell over. Carried indoors, he sat down on the sofa and died.

The Birmingham Coroner opened an inquest, at which a doctor testified that Adams had high blood pressure, along with chronic degenerative heart disease, which was so advanced that any sudden effort, strain or shock might have killed him. In addition, none of the superficial abrasions or bruises sustained in the contretemps with his neighbour were sufficiently severe to have caused his death.

Mrs Adams argued that although her husband had suffered from heart attacks two years ago, at the time of the alleged fight, his health was relatively good. She insisted that Bailey had punched her husband in the chest. Meanwhile, Bailey argued 'I never struck him at all. He had hold of me round the neck and we fell on the floor.'

With no consensus between the feuding neighbours, the coroner adjourned the inquest until 28th June to allow the police more time to make enquiries. In spite of the doctor's findings, Bailey was charged with manslaughter but was at least allowed bail to be with his new bride.

On 6th June, he appeared before magistrates, where all charges against him were dismissed. It appeared that he had simply had the misfortune to pick a quarrel with someone whose ill health made him likely to expire at the slightest provocation.

Coventry, Warwickshire

After a wedding at St Barnabas Church in Coventry on 23rd April 1938, the wedding party proceeded to the studios of photographer John Gillespie Clayton in Ford Street for the official photographs.

As the bride Lola Doreen Mitchell (nee Kendall) was being photographed, her husband noticed her dress touching an unguarded electric fire in the studio. The photographer's wife, Amy, was quick to move it away. However, as the five bridesmaids came forward to be photographed, there was a sudden scream. Bridegroom Charles Edward Mitchell looked round and saw twenty-three-year-old Eunice Naylor running towards him, her dress on fire. Mitchell ripped at the flaming fabric with his bare hands, stamping on the burning material, at which point, six-year-old Josephine Mary Russell ran over to try and help him. Her dress quickly caught alight, at which point pandemonium ensued.

Screams were heard by a bus conductor, who was sitting on his bus outside the studio at Pool Meadow. Seeing smoke issuing from the building, he scrambled over a low wall, where he saw two or three girls running around in a panic, burned but not actually on fire. Entering the studio, he found it well ablaze and filled with smoke and, not seeing any fire extinguishers, he bravely attempted to beat out the fire with a broom.

Eventually, nine of the wedding party were rushed to hospital and the studio was completely gutted. Only six-year-old bridesmaid Sheila Gunn escaped injury, although her dress was also burned.

The Grave of Eunice Taylor, by kind permission of Peter Barton

Eunice Naylor and Josephine Russell died from shock and burns soon after admission to hospital. The bride and another two bridesmaids were said to be in a critical condition, while Clayton and his wife, the groom and his brother, Thomas Mitchell, who acted as best man, were all treated for burns and released.

At the inquest on the deaths of the two bridesmaids, it was revealed that all of the bridesmaids' dresses had been made by the bride's mother from silk tulle, with taffeta underskirts. Mr Clayton tearfully told the coroner that everything happened so quickly, adding that it didn't seem like a normal fire but that the flames seemed to somehow leap from dress to dress. A verdict of 'accidental death' was recorded on both girls, the coroner bemoaning the fact that there were no fire extinguishers at the studio, while making it clear that he did not hold either Mr or Mrs Clayton criminally responsible for the tragedy.

Lola Mitchell, Josephine Hollier (8) and Leonie Kendall (16) remained in hospital, unaware of the fates of Eunice Naylor and Josephine Russell. Indeed, the bride was not informed of their deaths until her release from hospital on 14th May, when she was said to be distraught on hearing the news. Josephine Hollier was released from hospital on 29th May 1938, while Leonie Kendall was not discharged until just before Christmas, 1938.

East Midlands

Attenborough, Nottinghamshire

Alan Cuyler Grant-Dalton and Mr Philip S. Rook were both in the 504th (County of Nottingham) Bomber Squadron Auxiliary Air Force, the former a pilot officer and the latter a flying officer. Invited to the wedding of their friends John 'Jack' Soar and Janet Doreen Smith on 3rd November 1934, the two twenty-four-year-old pilots thought that it would be fun to fly to the wedding and drop confetti from their plane onto the happy couple.

Some of the guests were aware of the surprise and were looking for the plane's approach. When it was less than a quarter of a mile from the church, the Moth D.H. plane was seen to perform a perfect loop but as it prepared for a second, one of the wings seemed to crumple and bits began to fall off. The plane dropped like a stone and seconds later, it crashed into a field alongside Chilwell Manor Golf Course. Club professional Mr J. Lee ran to the wreckage along with several golfers who were playing the course at the time, but the plane was in flames and it was impossible to get close enough to rescue the two men, one of whom was still strapped in his seat, the other partly clear of the plane, as if he had made some efforts to jump out before impact.

The civil plane had been hired privately from Tollerton Flying Club and was in excellent mechanical order. Both Grant-Dalton and Rook were experienced pilots and, indeed, at least one had flown that particular plane before, only days before the crash.

At an inquest held by Nottingham District Coroner, Lieutenant-Colonel H. Bradwell, the jury returned a verdict of 'accidental death' on both men, remarking that it was extremely fortunate that, given the proximity of the golf course and the fact that debris was strewn in a radius of half a mile from the crash, the only other casualty had been a calf grazing in the field, which was killed outright. The Coroner expressed a view that the carrying of parachutes should be made compulsory on all civilian aircraft, adding that he believed that not carrying one was a court martial offence in the R.A.F. He was convinced that, had they had parachutes, both men would have survived the crash.

The remains of the two men were cremated, and their urns buried together in a single grave in West Hallam, Derbyshire.

Keyham and Billesden, Leicestershire

Fifty-four-year-old widow Mrs Kate E. Johnson was known in the village of Keyham as 'the bride who cannot get married.' In 1926, she had arranged three weddings in the space of one month but not one had come to fruition.

The first wedding should have happened on August Bank Holiday Monday. The ceremony was due to take place at Beeby and Kate had arranged to walk to the church with her bridegroom, George Kestin. However, Kestin failed to arrive to escort her and Mrs Johnson was forced to send her neighbour, Mrs Percy, to tell the vicar that the ceremony would not be taking place after all.

It was rearranged for 10th August but on this occasion, Mrs Johnson was taken ill, so Mrs Percy was pressed into service for a second time.

Third time lucky was to be on 23rd August 1926. The ring was bought, the wedding cake baked and the wedding breakfast prepared but again there was no Kestin, so Mrs Percy was sent to the vicar again. This time, Mrs Johnson went ahead with the reception without the bridegroom.

'I believe a third party prevented him from turning up' she told a local newspaper reporter, adding. 'It's not good enough to be fooled like this.'

Asked if she would be prepared to organise a fourth wedding, Mrs Johnson told the reporter 'I might.'

When Kestin was interviewed, he told the reporter that he was still willing to get married and to make Mrs Johnson a good husband. Kestin claimed that the first wedding didn't go ahead because Mrs Johnson's eighty-four-year-old mother raised objections. The bride was too unwell to attend the second ceremony and, as far as the third was concerned, he claimed that the couple had quarrelled after buying the wedding ring. 'I told her she need not put on her finery as I should not go to church', said Kestin.

He grumbled to the reporter about having to walk to Beeby in order to get married, saying that it would be much easier to have the wedding at Keyham. 'I have the ring at home' he stated 'and I am prepared to take out a special licence if she wishes. We could be very comfortable together'.

Mrs Johnson finally married at Billesden on 24th April 1927. After a brief courtship, she was led to the altar by seventy-year-old Freeman Allen, who had already buried two wives.

Hathersage, Derbyshire

In September 1905, John Ashton Eyre married Mary Madden at the Roman Catholic Chapel at Hathersage.

Unfortunately, Eyre's mother, Martha, was dead set against the marriage and made such a hue and cry in the chapel that she was eventually thrown out and the door locked behind her.

When the newlyweds left the chapel, they found all of John's belongings in a pile on the doorstep. The couple's wedding presents had been heaped on the ground by the chapel gate.

Note: Some contemporary newspaper reports give the bride's name as Miss Ward. Official records seem to indicate that Mary Madden is the correct name.

Newark, Nottinghamshire

On 6th June 1867, Catherine Alice Nicholson married Jonathon Hopkins Meredith at Newark. The bride's father was William Nicholson, an important local businessman and the owner of Nicholson's Ironworks, a large foundry in the town.

Nicholson's employees were keen to get involved in the celebrations. One of the products of the factory were large wrought-iron 'nuts', which were roughly three inches square, with a hole in the middle. These were placed on solid pieces of iron and gunpowder was placed in the central hole, after which an iron weight of 56 lbs or more was placed on top. When the gunpowder was lit, it made a tremendous bang like cannon fire, which could be heard all over the town and beyond.

Around twenty such devices had been lined up in front of the factory, between the outer wall and the tow path on the river. Firing commenced a few minutes before midday, with two or three being detonated in quick succession.

Men had been stationed at key points to keep the crowds safely at bay and, only when all of the devices had been fired and most of the factory workers had gone for their dinner did the works manager feel it safe to go back into the foundry and continue his work.

Unfortunately, one labourer wasn't ready to end the celebrations and decided to create another explosion using an anvil as a base, rather than the specially designed nuts. The anvil and the weight placed on top of it exploded, showering the area with large fragments of metal.

Fifteen-year-old Joseph Thomas Bailey, who had been watching the festivities, was struck on the chest by a particularly large fragment and died almost instantly. Eleven-year-old John Cooling was badly injured and was not expected to survive. Within minutes of the accident, the flags decorating the foundry had been lowered, the works closed and the ball planned for that evening in celebration of the wedding was cancelled.

An inquest held by Coroner R. Griffin heard that there had been no beer or intoxicating liquor at the factory. The jury later returned a verdict of accidental death on Bailey.

One of the local newspapers reported that part of Cooling's brain had been blown into his school cap. Yet it has proved impossible to find any newspaper reports of his death or of an inquest on his death hence it must be assumed that he survived.

Leicester, Leicestershire

On 13th April 1911, the morning of his wedding to Miss Ethel Slater, journalist Percy Havard Knight woke feeling unwell. He blamed his illness on the pork pie he had eaten the night before but after vomiting two or three times, he told his brother that he felt well enough to go into work for the morning.

Once in the offices of the *Leicester Mail,* twenty-nine-year-old Percy again complained of feeling ill, telling his colleagues he felt 'very seedy and giddy'. Noticing how pale he looked, his workmates advised him to go home but, after rushing off to vomit again, Percy claimed to be much better, saying that he '…felt champion'. Mere seconds later he began to stagger and collapsed in a chair, slumping forward over his desk and dying, less than three hours before his wedding.

Coroner Mr. E.G.B. Fowler opened an inquest at which Percy's brother Arthur shocked everyone present by informing the coroner that neither he, nor any member of his family, had any idea that Percy was intending to get married that day. Percy had been courting Miss Slater for ten years, even though his mother strongly disliked his girlfriend, describing her as 'flighty' and believing her unsuitable as a prospective daughter-in-law. The whole family had assumed that he had broken off the relationship in the face of his mother's disapproval of his choice.

However, the biggest shock was reserved for the doctor who had conducted a post-mortem examination on Percy and revealed that, while he had some minor signs of heart disease, he had died not from food poisoning but from poisoning by cyanide of potassium.

Both Percy and his brother were keen photographers and cyanide of potassium was used in the developing process. However, Arthur Knight insisted that they had not bought any for years and that there was none in the house. The day before his death, Percy had returned home from work for lunch and told his family that he had been in the darkroom at work. 'The fumes nearly choked me' he complained.

The coroner adjourned the inquest for a week to allow further investigations to be made and when the proceedings resumed, Miss Slater told the coroner that she had offered to break up with Percy as his mother was so against their courtship but Percy had been adamant, telling her. 'I am old enough and in a position to marry you and I am going to marry you.' Miss Slater told the inquest that, the night before their planned wedding, Percy had given her a wedding present and had seemed very content and cheerful.

Percy's mother, Elizabeth, admitted that she didn't approve of Miss Slater but contended that her son was a man and could make his own choices. 'I never said one word to deter him from marrying the young lady if he desired to do so' she insisted.

Medical evidence suggested that people did not normally die immediately from ingesting cyanide of potassium unless it was taken in very large quantities. When it was shown that Percy had bought cyanide of potassium the day before his death and that a wet glass bearing residue of the poison had been found in his office, the jury's verdict seemed a foregone conclusion, particularly as he had not yet purchased a wedding ring. Yet neither the coroner nor his jury seemed totally convinced that Percy had killed himself.

'Beyond the fact that the poor fellow's choice was disapproved by his mother, there seemed to be no motive for self-destruction', commented the coroner.

The jury eventually returned an open verdict, saying that, while Percy had died from ingesting cyanide of potassium, there was no evidence to show by whom it was administered. The jury added that, in their opinion, the mother and brother of the deceased had not told all they knew.

Derby / St. Pancras

On 9th April 1894, as the 11.55 Midland Express train from Derby to St Pancras raced through the countryside at fifty miles an hour, a number of hysterical women suddenly rushed into the smoking car claiming that there was a madman on board the train. Sir Thomas Roe M.P., who was travelling with his two nephews, immediately went to investigate.

The three men found a 'rough-looking' man in the dining car, fighting against three passengers who were trying desperately to pin him down, all the while '...uttering imprecations of the most violent kind.' He was raving and gesticulating wildly and had knocked over several tables and chairs in his struggles.

It transpired that forty-nine-year-old widower William Hodgkinson and forty-five-year-old widow Nellie Mackenzie had married only that morning and were on their way to St Pancras for a London honeymoon.

Bystanders felt that Hodgkinson should be put off the train at Luton, which was the next station. However, Roe pointed out that it would be inhumane to leave a bride in a strange, out of the way place with a mad husband. Hence the Hodgkinsons were moved to another carriage and kept confined until they reached London, where they were expecting to be met by Mr Hodgkinson's brother. At St Pancras, the police were informed of the incident and Hodgkinson was taken to a place of safety.

Matlock Bank (author's collection)

William was a former station master and licensed victualler, who had retired to a villa in Matlock Bank. According to his wife, he had not been drinking at all but a fit of madness suddenly overcame him during the train journey for no apparent reason.

Little Houghton, Northamptonshire

In December 1887, Mary Jane Deacon married Frank Dore at Little Houghton. After the wedding, the newlyweds and their guests went to the bride's parents' home, where a wedding breakfast had been prepared.

All went well until tea was served after the meal. Because they were catering for a total of twenty-two people, Mr and Mrs Deacon had borrowed a large urn in order to make the tea, but within minutes of drinking it, all of the guests began to feel unwell.

It was fairly obvious that they had been poisoned, since all twenty-two were vomiting and writhing in agony with stomach pains. A doctor was sent for and Mr Audland of Northampton Infirmary quickly traced the source of the poison to the tea urn, which had a copper top and a copper tap. Because it was used so rarely, copper had leached into the tea causing Verdigris poisoning.

Although all of the guests eventually recovered after treatment, the bride was particularly badly affected and the couple's honeymoon had to be cancelled.

Leicester, Leicestershire

The marriage between Miss Florrie Alexandra Squire and twenty-eight-year-old Co-Operative milk roundsman Harold Simpson was set to take place at St Saviour's Church, Leicester, on 12th September 1926 at eleven o'clock. However, at half-past seven that morning, Florrie received a note from her fiancé, delivered by his brother, that had been hastily scribbled on the back of an envelope: *'Dear Flo, can you lend me £10? If you can't, don't bother to get ready, because I am going to finish it all this morning. Yours forever, Harold'*

Florrie rushed round to Harold's house, to be told by his mother that he had just left home to go to her house. While Florrie was at his house, a neighbour came round to pass on a message to Mrs Simpson. Apparently, Albert had just telephoned her from Syston Station to ask her to tell his mother that he would not be coming home. The neighbour offered to fetch Mrs Simpson so that he could speak to her himself but Harold said that he couldn't wait as his train was just arriving.

Florrie had no alternative but to cancel the wedding arrangements. She had last seen Harold the evening before, when he was telling people how much he was looking forward to married life. The police were informed of his disappearance and made appeals in the newspapers for his whereabouts.

Simpson eventually wrote to his mother about two weeks later, saying that he was living in Camden Town, London, and working as a bar tender. Some of the contemporary newspapers hinted that a young, female Leicester hosiery worker disappeared on the same weekend but this has proved impossible to verify.

Note: There is some confusion regarding the prospective bride's name. Contemporary newspapers state that she is the adopted daughter of Mr and Mrs Squire, referring to her as Florrie Alexandra. Hence it is not clear if her surname is Squire, Alexandra or Alexander.

Walton-on-Trent, Derbyshire

Walton-on-Trent (author's collection)

On 1st January 1908, the village postmistress of Walton-on-Trent married the local saddler, after a courtship of thirty years.

One of their wedding presents was a live pig, which was duly bedecked in flowers and ribbons and taken to the church, where it squealed loudly, rampaged among the guests and staged numerous 'dirty protests'. It made such a nuisance of itself that it was eventually driven through the streets to the newlyweds' marital home, where it was bundled into a shed.

Kettering, Northamptonshire

It was bitterly cold on 2nd March 1940, the wedding day of twenty-year-old Vera Tyrell and Maurice Dunmore, who was also celebrating his twentieth birthday that day. Because of the cold, Vera decided not to wear her wedding dress but instead dressed in a much warmer outfit. Nevertheless, she caught a chill, which rapidly developed into pneumonia and she died in Kettering Hospital on 5th March.

Her husband had been at her bedside all the night before and, at one stage, she had asked him to play his piano accordion for her.

'Now I shall get better' she told him contentedly, as she closed her eyes and drifted off to sleep for the last time.

She was buried in the wedding dress she never got to wear.

Beeston, Nottinghamshire

On 12th June 1948, seventeen-year-old Sheila Chambers of Long Eaton should have been marrying twenty-two-year-old Reginald Lacey. Sadly, on what should have been her wedding day, she was mourning her fiancé, who had died at work the day before.

Lacey worked as an analytical laboratory assistant at Boots Pure Drug Co. Ltd at Beeston. Two days before his death, he went into the office of his supervisor, Mr A.W. Rideout, looking pale and anxious and asked him for an antidote to potassium cyanide. Apparently, he had been using the chemical to clean silver nitrate stains from his hands and realised too late that he had several small cuts on his fingers. Rideout applied the antidote and warned Lacey to wear rubber gloves in future when handling dangerous chemicals.

Two days later, on the eve of his wedding, another laboratory assistant heard Lacey call out from the laboratory. When he went to see what was the matter, he found Lacey slumped over the sink insensible.

Mr Rideout was sent for and he laid Lacey down on the floor and asked him if he wanted to vomit. When Lacey was unable to reply, Rideout sent for the factory surgeon and, while waiting for him to arrive, put his fingers down Lacey's throat to try and induce him to be sick. Sadly, Lacey died soon afterwards without ever regaining consciousness and a post-mortem examination conducted by Mr K. S. Dickenson found the cause of death to be cyanide poisoning. Dickenson theorised that Lacey had thrown some potassium cyanide down the sink, where it had come into contact with another chemical and released hydro-cyanic gas, which would have been fatal if inhaled.

At an inquest held by District Coroner Mr C.A. Mack, Lacey's workmates revealed that there had been three glass beakers in the sink, one that had recently been rinsed out, one containing an unidentified brown liquid and a third containing a partially dissolved solution of ferrous sulphate. Although potassium cyanide was only used very rarely in Lacey's department, a recently opened bottle was found nearby

Lacey's father told the coroner that his son was very hard-working, studious and keen to advance in his job. All the necessary preparations had been made for his wedding on Saturday and Reginald was very much looking forward to starting married life.

The coroner told the jury that they could rule out a verdict of suicide and accordingly a verdict of 'accidental death' was agreed upon. The coroner concluded by saying that, in his opinion, all dangerous chemicals in the department should be under stricter control.

Moira, Leicestershire

Twenty-six-year-old domestic servant Maud Freeman was said to be a strikingly pretty brunette with a particularly happy disposition. She was certainly highly regarded by her employers, consequently when she fell ill, shortly before her wedding to widower Tom Elmer of Burton-on-Trent, they sent her to Buxton for a few days to recuperate.

When she returned to her home in Moira, she was well on the way to recovery and plans went ahead for her wedding in September 1935. However, on the eve of the ceremony, Maud was apparently stricken with heart problems and collapsed, dying almost immediately.

Her fiancé was said to be grief stricken at the blow fate had so cruelly dealt him.

Mansfield, Nottinghamshire

On 15th December 1921 Ivy Avondale Johnson and Alexander Fraser Lobban were married at Mansfield. At their reception, they and their guests were listening to the best man reading out the many congratulatory telegrams, when the doorbell rang, announcing the arrival of yet another one.

Sadly, rather than a message of congratulations, this particular telegram was a notification that Lobban's father had died suddenly and unexpectedly. The wedding breakfast was immediately abandoned, as was the planned honeymoon in St Anne's-on-Sea, as the bridegroom rushed to Scotland to be with his family.

Peterborough, Northamptonshire

The marriage of Charles Hartley Taylor (22) and Norah Gladys Saul (19) at Lowestoft coincided with a heatwave. After their wedding, the couple headed off on their honeymoon, their first stop being rooms at Peterborough rented by Joseph and Kate Humphreys.

Kate was charmed by the couple, later declaring 'Altogether, a more loving couple never started on their honeymoon.' However, at half-past-four the following morning, the Taylors' apparent wedded bliss was shattered by four pistol shots.

Mr and Mrs Humphreys banged on their bedroom door, but the only response was an ominous gurgling noise. When the landlord and landlady tried to enter the room, they found the door had been barricaded from the inside with furniture.

Joseph Humphreys eventually managed to force an entry into the room, finding both Charles and Norah lying on the bed. Norah had apparently been shot three times in the back of the head and was barely alive. Her husband, who was still clutching a gun in his right hand, had blood pouring from his mouth.

Joseph ran for a policeman but such was the carnage inside the Taylors' bedroom, that the officer fainted on entering. Eventually, Charles and Norah were taken to hospital, both dying shortly after arrival.

A postcard was found in the room, on which Charles had written *'Communicate with Mike Taylor, 56 Radcliffe Road, S. Kensington and Robt. W. Saul, 7 Commercial Road, Lowestoft. Signed C. Taylor.'*

At an inquest on the two deaths, it was revealed that Norah had died from three gunshot wounds, while Charles had choked on his own blood, after putting the gun in his mouth and pulling the trigger.

Norah's father, Robert, told the inquest that the couple had been engaged for a year and had married with his blessing. Charles's demeanour towards Norah had always been 'lover-like' and, according to Robert, he was a steady and likeable young man, who had become like a son to his father-in-law. Letters received from Norah after the wedding gushed about how happy they both were to be married.

Charles was a man of private means and had no apparent worries, financial or otherwise. Indeed, the only possible explanation for his actions was advanced by a doctor, who told the inquest that '...suicidal and homicidal tendencies develop rather rapidly in hot weather.'

The inquest jury returned a verdict of wilful murder by Charles Taylor, who then committed suicide while the balance of his mind was disturbed.

Yorkshire

Dewsbury

In August 1905, domestic servant Annie Elizabeth Soothill met Arthur Asquith, who told her that he was the head gardener of a large manor house, Tweedale Hall in Dewsbury. Annie and Arthur courted for a few months before he proposed marriage.

The wedding date was set for 4th January 1906. Annie gave up her job in domestic service and rented a house to be their new marital home. Asquith assured her that he would furnish it and the furniture was expected to be delivered on 3rd January. When it did not arrive, he told Annie that their wedding must be postponed '...for a day or two'. He took her to the empty house, where they had planned to start their married life together, and kept her prisoner there for two weeks, giving her very little food.

He had already persuaded Annie to have the wedding presents delivered to their new home and on 13th January, he told her that the clock they had been given needed to be repaired and took it away. Two days later, he took a sewing machine, on the pretext of wanting to show it to his mother and he also removed the new cutlery from the house. He was later found to have pawned them, receiving ten shillings for the clock and cutlery and a further twenty-five shillings for the sewing machine.

Meanwhile, Annie's mother, who had no idea that her daughter wasn't married, came to visit the newlyweds. Asquith tried to persuade Annie to hide in the cellar while he got rid of her mother but Annie refused. Mrs Cox demanded to know what had happened to the missing wedding gifts and, when the man she believed was now her son-in-law was unable to give her a satisfactory answer, she went straight to the police.

When Detective Sergeant Charlesworth went to interview Asquith, he recognised him to be twenty-four-year-old miner Seth Jennings. Charged with theft of the wedding gifts, Jennings insisted 'I didn't steal them. She was present when I took them.'

Jennings was brought before magistrates at Dewsbury, where magistrate Alderman Kilburn described the case as '...the most heartless case possible for human ears to listen to.' Finding Jennings guilty as charged, Kilburn rued the fact that the maximum possible sentence he could award was six months hard labour at H.M.P. Wakefield, which the magistrate said hardly seemed adequate for '...the ruin of a decent girl and the degradation of a most respectable family.' To add insult to injury, Mrs Cox was obliged to repay the pawnbrokers a total of thirty-five shillings in order to get her daughter's wedding presents back.

Leeds

On Boxing Day 1925, bricklayer John William Dyer attended the wedding of his son, Alfred, to Agnes Ellaline Dooker. Once the ceremony was over, fifty-five-year-old Dwyer nipped into the church porch for a smoke. Unfortunately, while he was enjoying his cigarette, the wedding party left the church without him and he found himself locked in.

Shortly afterwards, a policeman heard somebody shouting and saw Dwyer standing inside Leeds Parish Church, his head sticking through a broken stained-glass window. John was later charged with wilfully damaging the window and appeared at Leeds Magistrates Court on 28th December to answer the charge against him.

Dwyer pleaded guilty, explaining that he had not intended to break the window but had knocked on it with his walking stick to try and attract attention to his predicament, since he didn't want to stay in the church until it opened again for services on Sunday. The case was adjourned for three months to allow Dwyer to pay for the cost of repairing the damage (about £5) at the rate of 5 shillings a week.

Bradford

On 6th June 1903, guests had assembled at Thornton Church, near Bradford to celebrate a wedding when the curate made an announcement. He told the wedding party that sadly the marriage couldn't take place that day as the register was locked in the church safe and the vicar, Reverend J. Jolly, had gone on holiday to Switzerland, taking the safe key with him.

While the sobbing bride was comforted by the guests, the groom and best man drove to consult Dr Robinson, the vicar of Bradford.

Robinson sent a workman back to the church with orders to break into the safe by any means. He also sent word that the curate must marry the young couple the next morning at eight o'clock. Sadly, most of the couple's forty-five guests had travelled from Lancashire to attend the wedding and were unable to extend their stay, so missing the ceremony altogether.

Dacre, Nidderdale

The wedding of thirty-year-old Enoch Horsman and Miss Louisa Mudd was arranged for 17th May 1905. The couple had been engaged for four years and in preparation for their married life, Enoch had purchased Deer Inn Farm at Dacre.

In the run up to his wedding, Enoch felt unwell for two or three days and his brother Tom told him 'Liven up or else you won't be able to get married.'

By the day before the wedding, he seemed back to his usual rude health. He worked on his father's farm until eleven o'clock in the morning, when he told his mother that he was going to take the horse and cart to his new home with a load of coal. When he didn't return for dinner, it was assumed that he had gone to visit his fiancée.

That afternoon, Tom went to fetch the cows in and, by chance, noticed his brother's coat lying on some thistles. When he went pick it up, he saw his brother sprawled face down in a small stream.

Tom pulled his brother from the water but he had obviously been dead for some time. The stream was normally about eight inches deep, but was occasionally dammed to make it easier for the cows to drink. Tom noticed that the stream had been freshly dammed with clods of earth, although he was later to say at the inquest on Enoch's death, that this would only have increased the depth by a couple of inches.

Enoch was found with his head and body in the stream but his legs on the bank at the side of the stream. The horse and cart that he was planning to use to transport coal were still in the barn at this father's farm.

The coroner established that Enoch was very much looking forward to his wedding. Asked if his brother might have committed suicide, Tom replied 'I never knew a happier lad. He had everything he asked for and everything he could wish and the best lass in all the Dales.' Enoch's mother told the inquest that her son was a '...fine, manly fellow' and that he had been his usual cheerful self before leaving the house.

Enoch had of course been unwell in the days before his death and had also suffered from occasional fainting and dizzy spells in the past. The way that he was sprawled on the bank suggested that he passed out and fallen face first into the stream. However, the fact that the brook was newly dammed and that he had removed his coat was more suggestive of suicide, even though he had shown no signs whatsoever that this was his intention.

The inquest jury eventually ruled that Enoch drowned himself, adding that there was not sufficient evidence to show the state of his mind at the time.

Naturally, his bride to be was devastated at hearing the news. The couple were very popular in the area and had received more than one hundred wedding presents. It proved impossible to notify the invited wedding guests and most turned up expecting to celebrate a marriage rather than to mourn Enoch's death.

Winksley, Near Ripon

Twenty-four-year-old Ronald Evans had grown up in Winksley but then moved away to Coventry, where he became a bus driver. On 21st April 1933, the evening before the wedding, he returned to Winksley to marry his childhood sweetheart, Rose 'Rosie' Victoria Carlin, after which they planned to live together in Coventry, where they had rented and furnished a house.

Since everyone at his fiancée's home was bustling about with last-minute preparations, Ronald and his future brother-in-law, Frederick, went to visit Ronald's parents. At around eleven o'clock that night, Frederick suggested that they should go and see how everyone was getting on at home, so Ronald jumped on the back of Frederick's motorbike and they set off to make the three-mile journey.

About an hour later, Frederick staggered through the door of his home with dreadful injuries. 'Go down the lane, you'll find Ronald hurt worse than I' he managed to say, before collapsing.

The Carlin family hastened to look for Ronald and soon came to the scene of the accident. There was a large cart at the side of the road, the driver of which was sitting sobbing on a bank. A policeman was already at the scene and, since Ronald was so badly injured, he refused to let the family see him. Both Ronald and Frederick were taken to Ripon Hospital, where Ronald died from a fractured skull on what should have been the morning of his wedding. Frederick had injuries to his neck, several broken fingers and concussion – he had apparently laid unconscious at the site of the accident for almost an hour before recovering sufficiently to summon help.

Coroner Colonel J. C. R. Husband opened an inquest and, after Evans had been identified, the proceedings were adjourned until

Frederick had been discharged from hospital and was well enough to give evidence.

When the inquest resumed, Frederick stated that he had been riding at 25 m.p.h. and accelerating, when he suddenly saw the stationery cart about three yards in front of him. There had been no time to brake and he had ploughed headlong into the cart, knocking the horse over.

Cart driver Thomas Johnson admitted to having had no lights on the cart. He had been on the road for many hours and had fully expected to reach his destination in daylight but had been given the wrong directions. Realising that it would be getting dark soon, he tried without success to borrow some lamps at a hotel. He had stopped on the side of the road to rest his horses, when he saw the motorcycle approaching at speed. He rushed to the front of the cart to try and warn the rider but Frederick obviously hadn't seen him.

The inquest jury believed that Johnson had done everything possible under the circumstances to try and prevent a collision. They returned a verdict of 'death by misadventure' on Ronald Evans, adding that they believed that the fact that the horse was knocked over indicated that the motorbike had been travelling at an excessive speed.

Hunslet, Leeds

On 4th September 1937, on the day he should have been marrying thirty-three-year-old Nellie Webber, Arthur Turpin was instead leading the mourners at her funeral, which took place in the same Leeds church where their wedding had been arranged.

Nellie acted as a housekeeper to her widowed father and on 1st September, she was cleaning the upstairs windows when she overbalanced and fell twenty feet, landing on her head. Although she was rushed to hospital, she died from a fractured skull soon after admission.

At an inquest on her death, Nellie's father, William, stated that she had been unwell recently and he had begged her not to sit on the windowsill while she was cleaning the windows for fear of having a dizzy spell. Nellie had ignored his advice.

Arthur Turpin was distraught, telling the inquest 'It's an awful loss to me. I can hardly believe it.'

Almost three thousand friends and neighbours attended the funeral, at which Arthur's tribute to his fiancée was a floral wreath in the shape of a broken harp, bearing the message 'From your broken-hearted sweetheart, Arthur.'

Batley Carr

Forty-nine-year-old William Henry Talbot's wedding to Mary Newsome was arranged for 18th February 1911. Early that morning, Talbot left his sister's home at Batley Carr, where he had been staying, telling her that he was going to have a shave and then call for his brother, who was to be his best man.

Mary and the wedding guests turned up at the church for the ceremony but there was no sign of the bridegroom and, after a forty-five-minute wait, the vicar was forced to cancel the service.

Meanwhile, Alexander Muir got talking to a stranger in a Bradford pub. They chatted and drank together for an hour, the man telling Muir that he had spent the whole day in Bradford and that he had been to the pantomime there that afternoon.

The man was Talbot and, when Muir left the pub, Talbot accompanied him. They made a brief stop at a chemist's shop, where Talbot purchased a bottle of phosphorous, which he said he wanted to kill rats in his cellar. The two men then caught a tram.

At the village of Carlingow, about two miles from Batley Carr, Talbot suddenly stood up. 'I am getting off here old chappie' he told Muir. 'Be good.'

Talbot's body was found four days later in a warm water dam at Wilson's Mill, Batley Carr, where the temperature of the water almost at boiling point. He was less than five minutes' walk from his sister's home.

An inquest on his death heard that he had been his normal happy-go-lucky self in the run-up to his wedding, although his fiancée did say that he had been a little quiet on the evening before. Everyone else believed that Talbot was looking forward to his wedding and had no worries, financial or otherwise. The inquest returned a verdict of 'suicide during temporary insanity.'

Goole

Shipyard labourer Arthur Thornton disappeared on the morning of his wedding to Miss Margaret Lewis, which was scheduled to take place at Goole Parish Church. Four days later, on 13th May 1908, his body was recovered from the water at Goole docks. In his pocket were a lady's gold wedding ring, a lady's watch chain and a gold locket containing a picture of his fiancée. There were also two letters, one written to him by her and the other his reply, which he had never posted.

At the inquest on his death, the coroner first read out the letter from Margaret to the deceased. '...*I feel as if I cannot call you dearest. I think you have forgotten that I am only a girl and not a hard-hearted man like you. I wrote [to] you because I thought my heart would burst and I did not think you would turn coward. You seem to make out that I am one of the street walkers in Goole, though I can hold my head a little higher than you can. It looks as if you have not one atom of love left in you, now that you have thrown me to the floor as far as you can. You have nearly broken my heart and you may as well finish it though I have a Dad who will not turn against me, I can no longer hold my head up.'*

Arthur's response showed his true feelings about his fiancée's pregnancy. *'Dearest, I did not deceive you when I did not seem pleased. I should have spoken my mind but it seemed very strange that you did not tell me of your trouble before. If it is the worst, then God help us for I am not prepared to meet it. I would sooner meet death. God grant that it may not be the worst. Every night from now my prayers will be said over and over again. I hope that God Almighty will deliver us from this delusion so that we may hereafter lead our own lives. I am spent up now, so with a stout heart, prepare at any moment. Heaven is my home. I close now with love and kisses, Arthur.'*

The coroner asked Margaret if Arthur had ever threatened suicide before and she admitted that he had done so in February of that year. She told the inquest that Arthur was with her almost all day on the two days before their planned wedding and had showed no signs of not wanting to go through with the marriage.

Asked how she thought that Arthur had met his death, Margaret told the coroner that he was very familiar with the docks and she couldn't believe that he had accidentally fallen into the water. She was convinced that he had taken his own life, rather than face up to the responsibilities of marriage and fatherhood.

The inquest jury were not so sure, stating that there was not enough evidence to conclude that Arthur Thornton killed himself. They returned a verdict of 'found dead.'

Sheffield

On 5th December 1937, two cars were involved in a head-on collision in a narrow lane at Richmond, near Sheffield. Both cars contained wedding parties and both weddings had taken place at St Mary's Parish Church Handsworth earlier that day.

One car contained brothers William and John Johnston, who had been to the wedding of their brother, Edward, to Maggie Austin. Both men sustained injuries to their heads and shoulders and William was trapped underneath the car, which overturned after hitting a lamp post.

The other car contained bride and groom Frank and Lilian Milnes (nee Kirk), the bridegroom's brother Edward, who had acted as their best man and two bridesmaids. They sustained only very minor injuries and shock.

Perhaps the most fortunate man was pensioner William Jenkinson, who was forced to jump over a wall into a garden to avoid being hit by Johnston's car.

William Henry Johnston (38) was later for summoned for reckless driving. He claimed to remember nothing at all after toasting the bride and groom at the wedding, having suffered a fractured skull in the crash. His brother, John Ogden Johnson (34) told the court that his brother was driving at no more than 30 m.p.h. However, his recollection of the accident differed from that of Frank Milnes, who claimed that Johnston's car was driving in the middle of the road '...at a terrific rate.' Milnes managed to stop his car but Johnston was unable to stop in time to avoid an accident and ploughed straight into him.

Johnston was defended by Mr J. W. Fenoughty, who claimed that the particular stretch of road where the accident happened was a death trap. The collision occurred at the bottom of a steep hill near a bridge and an S-bend, where the road narrowed from 27 feet to 17 feet. However, magistrates chose to believe Milnes' account and Johnston was fined £10 plus costs and his license was endorsed.

Tickhill

In September 1927, market gardener and small farmer William Orton Brown was invited to act as best man at a wedding in Tickhill. After the ceremony, the bride and groom were driving away when sixty-nine-year-old William decided to throw some confetti at them, stepping onto the running board of the moving car in order to do so. Unfortunately, he slipped and fell, banging the back of his head on the road.

William made light of his injury, brushing off the concerns of fellow guests at the wedding. He professed himself perfectly capable of walking a mile to his home but almost as soon as he got there, he died from a cerebral haemorrhage.

An inquest held by Doncaster District Coroner Mr F. Allen returned a verdict of 'accidental death.'

Selby

On 5th April 1904, coroner Major Arundel held an inquest at Selby Town Hall on the deaths of John Hodgson (32) and Henry Hall (19), who died at a wedding breakfast on 2nd April.

Hall's sister Sarah Ann was marrying Edward Ripley and, after the ceremony, the wedding party went to the bride's home at Cape's Yard, Ousegate, for the wedding breakfast.

The festivities began at about three o'clock in the afternoon and quickly degenerated into what the contemporary local newspapers described as '...a drunken orgie.' (sic). There was a barrel of spirits in the dairy, along with numerous bottles of port wine, whisky and rum lined up on the floor nearby.

At around eight o'clock in the evening, Hall, who was described as 'very drunk' went in search of more alcohol. He returned from the dairy brandishing a bottle and poured out glasses for himself, Hodgson and another guest, Eva Haigh.

Eva took the tiniest sip of her drink, thinking that it tasted funny. However, Hall and Hodgson threw back their drinks and within minutes, both had died, having mistaken a bottle of carbolic acid for whisky.

At the inquest, the coroner was told that the carbolic acid was kept on a shelf in the dairy, whereas the alcoholic drinks for the reception were on the floor. Hall was said to be so drunk as to be incapable of knowing what he was doing.

The inquest returned verdicts of 'misadventure, being under the influence of drink at the time' on both men.

Note: Some publications give the date of the wedding as 29th March 1904

Pontefract

In August 1924, magistrates at Pontefract ordered colliery worker James Hanson to pay his wife twenty-five shillings a week for deserting her.

Ivy Hanson (nee Gill) told magistrates that she and James were married on 23rd February 1924. Immediately after the ceremony, he put her on the bus to Knottingley, where her father lived, telling her that he would 'follow shortly'.

'He has not yet turned up' complained Mrs Hanson, adding that he had contributed only 6s 6d towards the upkeep of herself and their two children, one of whom had been born since the marriage. Hanson had continued to live with his mother in Pontefract, and had made no effort to make a home for his wife and family. He made no effort to turn up at the Magistrates' Court either and the judgement against him was made in his absence.

Barnsley / Sheffield

Twenty-one-year-old Nancy Watts and twenty-four-year-old Thomas Bartholomew were married on 10 May 1937 and, after the reception, best man Eric Hebden was supposed to drive them to Harrogate for their honeymoon. However, on the Barnsley to Sheffield road, the Riley car driven by Hebden was involved in a collision between a van and another car. Nancy was thrown out of the car and killed instantly, while several other people were injured. These included Doris Mundell, who had been travelling in Hebden's car, and James Crichton Terras, Ada Allott and William Hill, who were drivers of or passengers in the other vehicles involved.

Twenty-four-year-old radio salesman Hebden was arrested and charged with manslaughter and his case forwarded to the Assizes. Hebden remembered nothing at all of the accident. It was alleged by the prosecution that he was driving erratically and had approached a bend so fast that he was unable to control his car and had veered across the road into the path of the oncoming van, which mounted the footpath after the collision and ended up in a field. Hebden's car then rebounded into the path of a Hillman car, which was flipped onto its side by the impact. However, Thomas Bartholomew and a man named Eric Leather, who was driving behind Hebden's car at the time of the crash, both insisted that Hebden had not been speeding.

Hebden had drunk whisky, sherry and port at the wedding reception then returned home, where he felt 'unwell'. Hebden's father insisted that he was not drunk but suffering from stomach trouble. He had taken an emetic and, after vomiting, had slept for almost three hours before setting off to drive the bride and groom to Harrogate. Thomas Bartholomew also stated that Hebden was not drunk and none of those who had assisted in the aftermath of the accident had noticed any smell of alcohol in the car whatsoever.

Hebden was eventually found guilty of dangerous driving and of one count of causing bodily harm by wanton driving. Mr Justice Humphreys addressed him before sentencing, saying: 'One cannot be aware of the appalling loss of life caused by dangerous driving on the roads day by day, without realising that the time has come when persons must be punished who choose to take the risk of collision with another motor vehicle for their selfish pleasure, because it enables them to go a little bit faster than they would otherwise think it safe to do.' With that, Humphreys sentenced Hebden to four months' imprisonment and disqualified him from driving for five years.

Worsborough Bridge

When Percy Edwards married his sweetheart Violet Mitchell on 12th June 1916, his father was unable to attend the wedding, as he was a private in the 15th York and Lancs. regiment and was training in Blyth, Northumberland. However, the family were determined that he shouldn't miss out on all of the celebrations and soon after the ceremony, John's wife Elizabeth began to package up some cake and other foodstuffs to send to her husband.

Elizabeth's seven-year-old daughter Violet was watching her mother, as was a married daughter, Lily, who had attended the wedding. Six-year-old Lizzie was in the yard of their home at 26 Henry Street, Worsborough Bridge, picking up pieces of confetti, still dressed in the white silk dress she had worn for the wedding. Growing bored, Violet wandered into the kitchen, running back to her mother shouting 'Oh, mamma, our Lizzie's on fire.'

Mrs Edwards and Lily rushed into the kitchen, to find Lizzie completely enveloped in flames. They tried to beat out the blaze with their bare hands, before Lily fainted.

Their screams brought in neighbour Sarah Jane Stott, who managed to wrap the child in a rug and smother the flames. Dr

Beverley was sent for but he was out and his wife came in his stead to administer what first aid she could, pending her husband's arrival. Lizzie was rushed to Barnsley Hospital, where it was discovered that she was extensively burned all over her body, with the exception of a small area of her back. In deep shock, the little girl never rallied and died later that evening.

At an inquest held at the Town Hall in Barnsley, by coroner Mr P.P. Maitland, Elizabeth Edwards explained that the kitchen fire was very rarely used and had only been lit that day on account of the wedding breakfast. It was thought that Lizzie might have been trying to reach a comb on the mantlepiece, when her dress was caught by the unguarded fire.

The inquest jury recorded a verdict of 'accidental death.'

Attercliffe, Sheffield

On 8th January 1907, Miss Lena Hutchinson was married to petty officer first-class Francis H. Godfrey at Attercliffe, Sheffield. Before setting off to the church, Miss Hutchinson asked her father to pour her a glass of sherry to calm her nerves. However, nobody could find the corkscrew, so she eventually made do with a glass of port wine.

After the wedding, a reception was held at the home of the bride's parents, who had set up a table with port, rum, whisky, sherry, blackcurrant wine and ginger and peppermint cordials. The bride's two married sisters, Mrs Ada Battison and Mrs Kate Smith, asked their father to pour them each a glass of sherry.

Mrs Smith immediately noticed that her drink smelled 'funny' and took only a sip. Mrs Battison however, had no sense of smell and took a hearty swig of her drink. She immediately complained of a burning sensation in her mouth. 'If this is sherry, I will have no more of it. Take it back to the shop at once!' she exclaimed.

Within five minutes, Mrs Battison was vomiting violently and was semi-conscious. A doctor was sent for and he quickly determined that the 'sherry' was in fact benzine, a powerful irritant poison.

Initial reports in the contemporary newspapers suggested that two people died as a result of benzine poisoning. However, Kate Smith had taken only the tiniest sip of her drink and, although she was very unwell for a few days, Ada Battison fortunately made a full recovery.

All the drinks for the wedding had been bought from a local grocer's shop and stored in a cupboard until the wedding. The rogue bottle was clearly labelled sherry but had a slightly different cork to the other bottles. It was never established quite how the mix-up occurred.

Driffield

In June 1897, twenty-year-old Sarah Harper and twenty-four-year-old Fred Staves travelled from North Frodingham to Driffield to get married. Sarah was wearing a wedding dress and Fred was carrying the gold ring that he had bought for her, along with £12 that he had saved up, which he intended to use to furnish their marital home.

However, when the couple reached the Registry Office, Sarah had a change of heart and refused to go inside, telling people that Fred was '...a lazy fellow, who has nowt' and saying that she no longer wished to be married. Fred retired to a nearby pub to spend some of his savings, while Sarah went home alone.

Two days later, she changed her mind again and the couple went back to Driffield, where they were married.

Bentley

Twenty-year-old toffee factory worker Lily May Nunn and Albert Dixon, who worked on the surface of the Askern Main Colliery, had been courting for two years before their wedding on 7th June 1938 at the Church of Christ in Bentley, Yorkshire. The newlyweds enjoyed a reception at Bentley, before they and a handful of relatives went to a bus stop to wait for a bus to take them to their homes in Askern.

As the group waited for their bus to arrive, they heard a motorcycle approaching and before anyone could react, it ploughed into the wedding party, injuring both the bride and her father-in-law, who was also named Albert. Both were rushed to Doncaster Royal Infirmary, where Albert junior spent the night by his unconscious wife's bedside. At half-past ten the following morning, nurses suggested that the exhausted young man should go and try to get some sleep but he had only been at home for half an hour when he was summoned back to the hospital. Lily died from a broken neck soon afterwards, without ever regaining consciousness.

Her funeral was held at the church where she had so recently married, her husband placing the watch he had bought her as a wedding present in her coffin, along with a silver horseshoe she had been presented with at the wedding. By tragic coincidence, the day of her funeral should have been her wedding day – the couple were forced to bring forward the date because of a mix up with the arrangements.

Sheffield

Lizzie Baxter was due to marry Joseph Bradshaw on 21st June 1898 and had hired a carriage for the journey from her home to St Andrews Presbyterian Church, Sheffield. Lizzie was terrified of horses and so made sure to ask for a driver that she had used before and trusted. Even so, when she climbed into the carriage, she pleaded with driver George Hardwick 'George, please don't drive very fast'. Hardwick assured her that he would go nice and steady.

Lizzie climbed into the carriage with her uncle, John Brown Corrie, who was to give her away and her bridesmaid, her twelve-year-old niece Jennie Ellis. Hardwick was standing by the horses' heads, steadying them but before he could climb onto the driving seat, the horses suddenly moved off.

The bride's house was at the top of a very steep hill. Using the reins, Hardwick managed to steer the horses into a wall but, as they jerked to a sudden halt, the reins were snatched out of his hands and he fell flat on his back. Finding themselves free, the two horses set off at a gallop.

In the carriage, thirty-four-year-old Lizzie flew into a panic. She opened the carriage door as if to leap out but her uncle seized the back of her dress and held on tightly, begging her not to jump. Lizzie continued to plead with her uncle to let her go and as the carriage began to slow down at the bottom of the hill, he decided that he should release his hold, rather than risk her being seriously injured should the carriage overturn. Telling Lizzie to jump towards the footpath he let go of her dress and she sprang from the carriage, landing on her back.

The thirty wedding guests were already at the church awaiting the arrival of the bride. Told of the accident, Bradshaw rushed to his Lizzie's home, finding her semi-conscious. At first, she appeared to have suffered nothing more serious than badly bruised elbows but that night her condition worsened and she died the following morning. John Corrie and Jennie Ellis stayed in the carriage until it crashed into a wall and sustained only minor injuries.

Coroner Mr Dossey Wightman later held an inquest on her death at The Nottingham Hotel, Sheffield. John Corrie told of the dilemma he faced in trying to decide if it was better for Lizzie to jump out of the runaway carriage or for her to risk serious injury should it overturn. When the carriage began to slow, he decided on the former option, possibly unwisely in view of his survival.

It was rumoured that the barking of a small terrier dog had startled the horses, yet Corrie had not heard it. Having been driven by Hardwick before, he knew him to be a steady and reliable driver and claimed that, until the moment that they bolted, both horses had been calm and collected.

The coroner was obviously sensitive to Corrie's feelings and refrained from any suggestion that he had made the wrong decision in allowing his niece to jump. He returned a verdict that Lizzie was '...accidentally killed by jumping from a carriage through a pair of horses running away.'

Harrogate

On 9th March 1891, twenty-eight-year-old Leonard Harrison married nineteen-year-old Hilda Harland. The couple parted company at the church door, Harrison returning to his home in Hull and his bride to her mother's house.

In 1905, Harrison applied for a divorce, stating that he and his wife had never lived together after their marriage. The couple had first met in 1887 and become engaged in 1889 but their engagement was unhappy and the pair frequently argued. However, once the bride's mother discovered that they had been intimate during their relationship, she insisted that they should get married and nothing would dissuade her. Eventually Harrison and Hilda agreed to go through with the ceremony but separate at the church door, being married in name only.

In due course, Hilda started a career as an actress and met fellow actor Alfred Hodgson, a.k.a. Alfred Paunice. She and Alfred began living together, leading her husband to petition for a divorce, citing Hodgson as co-respondent. Harrison was granted his *decree nisi*.

Jump

Clara Ellis and Robert Ernest Machin were married at Dewsbury Registry Office on 1st January 1921. After the ceremony, they were returning home to the village of Jump with two friends, Hugh and Frances Jenkins, in a car driven by Arthur Dyer.

The car was being driven slowly through the village and, as Dyer approached a bend, he sounded his horn twice. Clara Machin recalled, seeing a horse's head – the next thing she remembered was being taken to the home of Dr Barclay Wiggins with her husband, who was unconscious.

Having examined Machin, Dr Wiggins came to the conclusion that he was so badly injured that it wasn't worth sending him to hospital, suggesting instead that he was taken home.

Machin died within minutes and, at the inquest on his death, the coroner was told that although the only external injury on his body was a small square bruise on the left-hand side of his chest, he had suffered terrible internal injuries. Dyer's car had been in collision with a horse and flat cart being driven in the opposite direction by Robert Gooder, who admitted to taking the bend wide. Although Gooder had swerved to the right to try and avoid the collision, his horse had reared up in fright and the left-hand shaft of the cart had penetrated the car bonnet and impacted with Machin's chest. He had suffered three broken ribs and the ends of the bone had punctured his lung and the outer wall of his heart, causing massive and fatal internal bleeding.

The inquest returned a verdict of 'accidental death', the coroner censuring Gooder and telling him that if he had been driving on the correct side of the road, the accident would never have happened.

Sheffield

Michael Sweeney and Elsie Russell married on 11th November 1928 and had their reception at a pub in Sheffield. The celebrations then continued at the bride's father's house but were rudely interrupted by the arrival of an uninvited gate-crasher.

Thirty-five-year-old Ernest Ashley was very drunk and his first act on arriving at the party was to go into the kitchen, where he assaulted the bride. He was eventually given a cup of beer, which he downed in one before smashing the cup.

He then twice assaulted Harriet Oxley, one of the wedding guests, once in front of her boyfriend. He was asked to leave by the bride's father, Charles William Russell, at which he kicked Russell, breaking his ankle.

At Sheffield Magistrates' Court, Ashley insisted that he had gone to the party at the invitation of another man, although he couldn't recall who had invited him or accompanied him there. He claimed to have been kicked up and down the street by at least twenty people after being ejected from the party and was eventually found by a policeman lying unconscious in the gutter, bleeding from a head wound.

The magistrates had little sympathy for him, sentencing him to one month's hard labour for being drunk and disorderly, two months' hard labour for assaulting Harriet Oxley and six months' hard labour for assaulting Mr Russell, the sentences to run concurrently.

North East

South Shields, Tyne and Wear

In April 1891, a marriage was solemnised at the Registrar's Office in South Shields. The bride, Lady Mite, was just 32 inches tall, while the bridegroom, a solo euphonium player named Professor Hedley, stood 6'1" tall. The man who gave the bride away was Monsieur Hubert, a man without arms, who signed the register as a witness holding the pen between his teeth. The best man was Captain Dallas, who was 7'1" tall and the bridesmaids included an American giantess named Nina, who weighed more than 44 stones. The wedding party and their guests were all members of Wombwell and Bailey's menagerie and circus, who were appearing at Houghton-le-Spring. Their wedding presents included a Pullman living wagon from Messrs Wombwell and Bailey.

Gateshead, County Durham

Twenty-two-year-old John Hudson White was due to be married on 7th April 1928, at two o'clock in the afternoon. In order to finish work at midday and have time to prepare for the ceremony, John changed his shift at Allbusen's Works, a part of the Imperial Chemical Company.

That morning, his workmates heard a terrible scream and, when they rushed to investigate, they found that John's clothing had become caught in machinery and he had been dragged between two heavy rollers of a crushing machine. The machine was quickly stopped but by the time he was extricated, John was dead.

Coroner Mr A. E. E. Boulton later recorded a verdict of 'accidental death.'

Alnwick, Northumberland

After their wedding on 5th April 1937, Robert Drummond and his bride Jane (nee Tait) went to visit his sister in Sunderland Street, Newcastle. Mrs Allen lived on the second floor of a tenement and, as they arrived, Robert told Jane to go on alone as he needed to visit the lavatory in the back yard.

In order to get to the lavatory, Robert had to walk down some steep stone steps. When he did not arrive at Mrs Allen's rooms, Jane went to see what had happened to him and found him lying at the bottom of the steps.

'What's the matter?' she asked him, to which her husband replied 'Nothing.'

Robert was unable to stand up and Jane was unable to lift him, so she enlisted the help of her brother-in-law. When Mr Allen finally got Robert upstairs, he was conscious and talking but appeared to be bleeding from his ears. It was decided that he should spend the night at his sister's house, while Jane went back to their marital home alone.

The Drummonds were supposed to be going to Alnwick for their honeymoon but the following day Robert was still feeling unwell, complaining of nausea and a bad headache. Jane tried to persuade him to call a doctor but he refused, saying that he would be fine the next morning and, if necessary, would consult a doctor at Alnwick.

The next morning, Robert travelled to Alnwick by train. He vomited during the journey and when he disembarked at Alnwick Station, he was staggering as if drunk. He had known station porter John T. Hopper all his life, yet when Hopper spoke to him, he didn't recognise him.

'Have you been drinking?' Hopper asked him.

'No, I have a bad head and a queer feeling' Robert replied.

Hopper realised that there was something badly wrong with Drummond and took him straight to Alnwick Infirmary. There he quickly lapsed into unconsciousness and, on 14th April, he died.

A post-mortem examination pinpointed the cause of death as laceration of the brain and haemorrhage from the right middle meningeal artery.

At the inquest on forty-two-year-old Drummond's death, Deputy Coroner Mr J.W. Sylvester expressed surprise that he had been able to continue walking and talking for three days after the fall that caused such catastrophic injury to his brain. Dr Welch, who had performed the post-mortem explained that the meningeal artery was not completely severed – had it been, Drummond would have died within a few hours of the fall.

The inquest jury returned a verdict of 'accidental death.'

Sunderland, Tyne and Wear

On 27th July 1907, twenty-eight-year-old chauffeur Oswald Stephen Wardroper was a guest at a wedding, and afterwards at the reception held at The Empress Hotel, Sunderland.

Towards the end of the evening, the wedding guests gathered in the hotel coffee room. Wardroper left the room and, a few minutes later, another guest, Rebecca Shapp met him coming down from the upper floor.

'Are you going back to the coffee room?' she asked, to which Wardroper answered that he was. Then, to Rebecca's surprise, he suddenly lay across the bannister on his stomach and began to slide downstairs. Moments later, there was a loud thud as he fell head first off the bannister and plummeted to the lobby below, sustaining fatal head injuries.

An inquest on his death held by coroner Mr Burnicle at Sunderland Infirmary determined that Wardroper had died an accidental death due to concussion of the brain caused by the fall. It was particularly noted that he was a teetotaller, who had not consumed so much as a single drop of alcohol that day.

Hetton-le-Hole, County Durham

After the death of her husband, Margaret Addison of Hetton-le-Hole was left with four young children to raise. She took in a lodger, farm labourer John William Johnson, who quickly became like one of the family. Numerous times throughout the years, Johnson asked Margaret to marry him but she always refused.

In 1891, Margaret's son got married and brought his wife to live at his mother's home. Suddenly, there was no room for Johnson and, after fifteen years, he was asked to leave. He was not happy to do so, complaining to anyone who would listen 'After I have helped bring her family up, to throw me off now.'

To make matters worse, once Johnson had moved out, Margaret began courting a man named Andrew Simpson and before long, a wedding was arranged. Her former lodger was terribly affronted, telling people that he would 'do for her' and that there would be a funeral before there was a wedding. When he was urged not to do anything hasty, he insisted 'I'm not scared of the rope.'

On the morning of 31st October 1891, Margaret left home to meet Simpson for their wedding. She had not walked far when someone tapped her on the shoulder and, as she turned to see who it was, Johnson lifted a revolver and shot her in the head. Witnesses heard her say 'Stop it!' before he pulled the trigger again and she fell to the ground, mortally wounded.

As soon as he had ascertained that she was dead, her murderer turned on his heel and walked to the village Police House. Sergeant Cartwright was not at home, so Johnson told his shocked wife Sarah 'I have shot my landlady.' With great presence of mind, Sarah opened a cell door and he walked calmly inside, handing Sarah a revolver, three bullets, his purse and a knife as she shut the door.

John William Johnson was charged with wilful murder and appeared before Mr Justice Wills at the Durham Assizes on 2nd December. He insisted on pleading guilty, assuring the judge that he fully understood what he was doing and had no desire to be defended. This left Wills no alternative but to pronounce the death sentence.

Johnson was executed by James Billington at Durham Prison on 22nd December 1891. He went quietly and calmly to the gallows, saying 'Into thy hands I command my spirit' as the hangman slipped the hood over his head.

Note: Johnson's name is given as William Johnson in many of the contemporary newspaper reports on the tragedy. Records suggest John William Johnson is correct.

West Hartlepool, County Durham

As the date for twenty-five-year-old Madeline Rawling's wedding to Edgell Stilwell drew nearer, the young woman viewed that event with a mixture of excitement and trepidation. Stillwell worked for the Civil Service and, immediately after the ceremony, he and his new bride were to be posted to Borneo. While Madeline loved her fiancé and wanted to get married, the idea of leaving her home and family worried her greatly and she grew ever more despondent.

On the eve of her wedding on 18 December 1909, Stillwell was reading in the drawing room of his fiancée's home when he heard her calling him from upstairs. When he went to see what she wanted, he found her standing before the mirror in the guest bedroom. 'Will you forgive me?' she asked him, adding 'I have taken poison.'

Madeline's father was a doctor. He was unwell at the time and sleeping but when roused by her sisters, he quickly administered an emetic. The family doctor was summoned and administered strychnine, in an effort to counter the effects of the carbolic acid that Madeline had drunk. When that had no effect, he attempted artificial respiration but Madeline died without regaining consciousness.

Madeline was said to have a bright, cheerful disposition and an unfailing kindness of heart. While she undoubtedly loved her husband-to-be, the coroner speculated that she was unable to bear the wrench of leaving her family, returning a verdict that she died '…from poison, self-administered during mental depression.'

Wallsend, Tyne and Wear

Wallsend (author's collection)

On 6th October 1928, the morning of his wedding, Frank Stephen Dryden appeared at his fiancée Elizabeth Border's house covered with mud and in an exhausted condition. Having told her and her mother that he had saved up £27 for the wedding, he now claimed that, having withdrawn his money from the bank, he had been set upon and robbed of his life savings.

The robbery was reported to the police, who arrived at the church just after the conclusion of the ceremony to interview him. However, Frank gave several conflicting accounts of the robbery and ended up being arrested himself.

It emerged that Frank had indeed saved up £27 but he had then frittered it away and was too ashamed to tell his wife-to-be and her mother. Hence, on his wedding day, he went to the Newcastle Savings Bank shortly after midday and demanded money, placing his right hand in his pocket to suggest that he had a gun.

Bank manager Peter Grant Munro courageously refused to hand over any cash. Instead he heaved a desk at the robber, who staggered momentarily before fleeing, with Munro in hot pursuit shouting 'Stop that man! He has tried to rob the bank.'

Passer-by Ernest Latty, an aircraftman in the R.A.F. attempted to rugby tackle Dryden, who escaped after a brief struggle.

Dryden appeared at Newcastle Assizes, charged with demanding money '...feloniously and with menace.' The jury found him guilty but, as he was previously a man of good character, he was sentenced to only nine months' imprisonment.

Chester Le Street, County Durham

Fifty-two-year-old widower John Thomas Robinson had been courting widow Ethel Holt for more than three months when he proposed marriage to her. The wedding was fixed for 6th October 1928, at Chester Le Street Registry Office. Unfortunately, on the night before the wedding, Joh had not yet plucked up the courage to break the news of his impending nuptials to his six children from his first marriage.

On the morning of the wedding, twenty-one-year-old William Robinson went to the Labour Exchange to sign on. When he returned, his sister Olive told him that their father had not yet got up and that he had not replied when she called upstairs to wake him. William went to his father's bedroom and, receiving no response to his knocks on the door, he went inside, finding his father sprawled across the bed with his throat cut, an open razor clenched in his left hand. William called the police and a doctor but his father's body was cold and he had obviously died some hours earlier.

At an inquest held by coroner Mr R. E. E. Boulton, William stated that he had heard his father come downstairs for a drink of water at about a quarter past eleven the night before his death. He had then neither seen nor heard anything of his father until finding him dead the following morning.

Ethel Holt told the inquest that she had seen her fiancé on the night of 5th October, when they had eaten supper together. At that time, John seemed his usual cheerful self, and was very much looking forward to his wedding. However, according to Ethel, only a few days before, John had told her that he had thought about cutting his throat, saying that he would probably have done so if it wasn't for her. Finally, Ethel told the coroner that John was always complaining about his children, saying that they never did anything for him.

The inquest found that Robinson committed suicide, adding that there was insufficient evidence to indicate the state of his mind at the time.

South Shields, County Durham

On 13th September 1904, the afternoon before her wedding to twenty-three-year-old Mr Evelyn Wood, twenty-two-year-old Mary

Evelyn Redmayne walked out of her home at South Shields. She left behind a note, in which she revealed that she couldn't go through with the wedding. '*I have gone away. Do not try and trace me*' concluded the note.

Mary took a train to Newcastle, then another to the small village of Craighill, where she arrived unexpectedly at the house of some friends. She stayed with them overnight, telling them that her wedding had been postponed and that she had been 'sent away'. As she had no luggage with her, her friends were suspicious but before they could make enquiries of her family, Mary left their house and took another train, this time arriving at the home of relatives in Selside, Yorkshire.

Once again, she told the same story of a postponed marriage, adding that she was on her way to visit her brother in the Philippines. This time, her relatives were able to send a telegram to her mother, who set out as soon as possible to collect Mary and bring her home.

Mary had eaten very little food during her wanderings and was weak, confused and exhausted, recalling absolutely nothing of the past couple of days. Once she got home, her family doctor diagnosed mental aberration due to over excitement and ordered her to have complete rest and quiet for a week.

It is reported that the jilted bridegroom went for a holiday in the country. Records show that he eventually married another woman in 1907, while Mary married in 1909.

Blyth, Northumberland

Thirty-eight-year-old pit deputy James Donohoe Jones, who was widely known by the nickname 'Pom', was a widower with three children aged three, twelve and seventeen.

In April 1952, Henry Norman Hall and his wife Edith were on board the Blyth Ferry when they met up with Pom and quickly realised that he and Edith had gone to school together. A friendship developed between the three but as time passed, Hall began to suspect that Edith's feelings for Pom were a little more than friendly. When Edith and Pom were seen kissing, Hall became jealous, in spite of his wife's assurances that her feelings towards their friend were merely brotherly. An argument ensued and Edith told her husband that if he couldn't trust her after seventeen years of marriage and four children then she didn't want to be with him. Edith stormed out of the marital home but returned four days later and promptly tried to commit suicide by taking thirty aspirin tablets. Although very unwell, she refused to allow her husband to call a doctor, saying that she was too ashamed to face anyone.

Soon afterwards, Hall called a policeman to his home, believing that P.C. Middleton had witnessed Jones either raping or sexually assaulting Edith in a field. P.C. Middleton reassured Hall that he had only seen Edith and Pom sitting together on a grass verge but Hall refused to be pacified. 'I will make that ******* pay for this if it's the last thing I do' he ranted. Middleton advised him not to do anything, as he would get himself into trouble. 'I will overlook it this time and give her another chance' Hall promised.

On 14th May 1952, widow Martha Ellen Burt moved into the area and she and Pom began courting. The courtship progressed quickly and on 30th July, Pom and Mrs Burt were married at the Registry Office in Morpeth. After the ceremony, they went to the Ridley Arms Hotel in Cambois to celebrate.

Unfortunately, Hall and his wife were already at the pub. Pom ordered drinks for everyone and two were taken to the table where the Halls were sitting. As soon as he heard who had bought them, Hall told barmaid Doreen Silverton to take them away. He later went to the bar and purchased two bottles of beer, putting one in his pocket, intending to take it home. He asked his wife if she would prefer to go to another pub but she refused.

As the barmaid flicked the pub lights on and off to signal last orders, Hall beckoned to Pom, who followed him out to the pub toilets. Hall was heard to say 'You have insulted my wife. We are going to settle it now'. The two men began to scuffle, Hall shouting 'You took my wife down'. Minutes later, Pom was found staggering along a passage outside the pub's toilets, blood pumping from his face and neck. He died within minutes and a post-mortem examination later found that his jugular vein and a major artery in his neck had been severed.

By now, Hall and his wife had left the pub but, having spoken to those customers who had witnessed the fight, the police went straight to his home. Hall's clothes were heavily blood stained and, when he admitted to having fought with Jones that evening, he was arrested and taken to Blyth Police Station, where he was charged with murder.

Hall was eventually sent for trial at the Northumberland Assizes, where he pleaded not guilty. (Before the start of the trial, he officially objected to the presence of three female jurors, and there was a slight delay while male replacements were found.)

Evidence was given that Jones's injuries were consistent with being hit by a bottle. A broken beer bottle was found in the pub toilets and it was deemed impossible for Jones to have fallen on it accidentally. As far as the prosecution was concerned, the jury could only find Hall guilty of wilful murder, since nothing justified the use of a bottle in a fight.

On his arrest, Hall had been examined by a doctor at Blyth police station. The doctor found just one small, rather insignificant, abrasion on his upper lip – he had no other injuries and certainly none on his knuckles or hands to indicate his involvement in a fist fight.

Hall denied having beckoned Jones to go outside with him, claiming instead that he had merely asked him if he might have a private word. He intended only to speak to Jones but, before he could do so, Jones hit him in the face. The bottle of beer that Hall had bought to take home was in his pocket and, as the two men scuffled, he felt Jones take it out. Seeing Jones raise his arm to hit him with the bottle, Hall said that he threw up his arms in self-defence. As he did so, he accidentally smashed the bottle in Jones's face.

The prosecution counsel told the jury that they would probably never hear a less convincing story, adding that it must have grieved Hall sorely to see his arch enemy Jones so happy on his wedding day but Hall's defence argued that Jones's death had not been premeditated and that Hall had intended nothing more than to defend his wife's honour.

Mr Justice Gorman spent a long time addressing the jury, ensuring that they fully understood the legal difference between murder, manslaughter and self-defence. The jury deliberated for seventy-five minutes before returning to find Hall guilty of manslaughter, on the grounds that he had been subject to a great deal of provocation. Gorman took this into account, sentencing Hall to seven years' imprisonment.

Seaham Harbour, County Durham

After their wedding ceremony on 4th September 1937, Eileen and Sidney Davis spent the evening with Sidney's mother, who had been around to the flat they had rented in Seaham Harbour earlier that day to clean it for them. Mrs Davis told them that she had smelled gas while at the property but had opened a window and the smell had soon dissipated.

When Eileen and Sidney went to the flat, they too could smell something unusual but thought that it was the new linoleum that had recently been laid. Both were smokers and, after enjoying a cigarette, they went to sleep in their marital bed for the first time.

They newlyweds were supposed to have dinner with Mrs Davis senior the next day but didn't turn up. Mrs Davis went to their flat but there was no response to her knocks on the door and she assumed they had gone out for the day. She went back to the flat the following morning but again, nobody answered the door. Eventually, she voiced her concerns to neighbours, who broke the door of the flat down, finding both Mr and Mrs Davis unconscious in their bedroom. Both had been gassed and twenty-eight-year-old Sidney Davis failed to regain consciousness and died that day in hospital.

Eileen Davis could recall nothing at all after smoking a cigarette with her husband on their wedding night until she woke up in hospital to learn that he had died. She was later to sue landlords John Foots and his wife Alice for the sum of £350 for injuries to herself, the death of her husband and his funeral expenses. The case was heard at the Durham Civil Assizes by Mr Justice Wrottesley.

Gas fitter Mr Miller was called to make the premises safe after Mr and Mrs Davis were taken to hospital and found that most of the escaping gas had dispersed up the chimney, hence no explosion had occurred when the couple had their cigarettes before sleeping. Miller had turned the mains gas supply on at Mr Davis's request on the day of the wedding. He told the court that he had checked the meter several times, to ensure that there was no movement that might indicate an escape of gas inside the property.

It emerged that, when Mr and Mrs Davis initially looked at the flat with a view to renting it, there had been a gas fire in the bedroom. Mrs Davis had told the landlords that they didn't need it and so the Foots asked their son Edward to remove it.

In court, Edward insisted that, having removed the gas fire, he had left a tap on the pipe and his father-in-law John Potter corroborated his account, having helped him take away the fire. However, the tap had mysteriously disappeared and, since the build-up of gas that killed Davis occurred because of an open-ended gas pipe, the judge found for Mrs Davis and awarded her the full amount of her claim.

The Foots appealed the decision and were successful in getting it reversed. At the Court of Appeal, Lord Justice Mackinnon, Lord Justice du Parcq and Mr Justice Bennett agreed that there had been no formal undertaking by the Foots to remove the gas fire for their new tenants and thus no undertaking for them to use reasonable care and skill while doing the job.

North West

Higher Ardwick, near Manchester, Lancashire

Clerk Thomas Clemson Wilde (30) married Mary Sutherland at Higher Ardwick near Manchester on 21st September 1905. The couple had planned to honeymoon in Blackpool for a week from Monday 25th September.

On 23rd September, Thomas had a business appointment. He seemed in a particularly cheerful frame of mind and his last words to his wife before leaving home, were about their planned holiday, saying how much he was looking forward to it.

When Thomas failed to return home that night, Mary feared that he had been in an accident. She contacted police and the local hospitals but there was no news of her missing husband until the following morning. When she should have been travelling to Blackpool for her honeymoon, Mary received a postcard from her husband, which read: *'My dear wife, I am sorry to have to spoil what would have been a happy married life but I have got into trouble through being good to others. I expected this month £200 and all through this I am not able to pay my way. Don't be down-hearted, although it is the worst that could happen. I know neither you nor anyone else will forgive me for this, Good-bye, CLEMSON.'*

Wilde's body was found later that day in the sea near Blackpool. An inquest on his death was held at Lytham-St-Anne's, where Mary told the court that she and her new husband were very happy and she had never imagined that he would leave her in this way after only two days of marriage. The inquest jury found a verdict of 'suicide while of unsound mind.'

Salford, Lancashire

Thirty-four-year-old Frank Crombleholme appeared at Salford Police Court on 15th February 1934, on what should have been his wedding day.

He was sentenced to twelve months' imprisonment for robbing his landlord of jewellery valued at £16, £50 in cash and a Manchester Corporation Bond worth £500. He was further charged with obtaining £50 by false pretences and with stealing an additional £20 in cash. His fiancée was in court and sobbed after hearing the sentence.

The prosecutor, hairdresser Ernest Johnson, had kindly taken Crombleholme into his house in November 1930, when he was destitute. Cromblehome obtained £50 from Johnson by falsely claiming that he had secured a job with a clothing club but couldn't afford the deposit that the firm wanted against supplying him with stock for his business.

To support his claim, Crombleholme paid a Manchester office one shilling to compose and type two letters, one purporting to have been written by Mr Johnson and the other by the clothing company. In Crombleholme's defence, Mr Kenneth Burke stated that his client believed that his business venture would be successful and fully intended to repay his landlord but the magistrates took this with a pinch of salt.

Mr Johnson was aware of the fraud some time before he brought the prosecution against his lodger but delayed the process because his own parents were ill and he didn't want to upset them. However, when Crombleholme broke into Johnson's shop and stole £20, it was the last straw.

Records show that Crombleholme married a Miss Ethel M. Clark in April 1935, presumably after serving his prison sentence.

Manchester, Lancashire

While attending a wedding reception in the slum district of Manchester in April 1904, forty-nine-year-old Mary Cook was found at the bottom of the stairs, bleeding heavily from her nose. She was taken to hospital, where it was initially believed that her injuries were consistent with an accidental fall but when she regained consciousness, Mary made a statement, alleging that the bridegroom, Tommy Sparkes, had kicked her, choked her and then thrown her downstairs.

Mary died soon after making this statement and, at the inquest, Sparkes denied having anything to do with her death, claiming that he and his wife had retired to their bedroom by the time she fell downstairs.

Both Sparkes and his wife were said to be very, very drunk at the wedding breakfast, while Mary herself had apparently drunk enough to make her unsteady on her legs. The coroner suggested that both Mr and Mrs Sparkes were most probably too drunk to have any clear recollection of the evening and, at his suggestion, the jury returned an open verdict.

Chester, Cheshire

When gunner Gilbert William Whitley met Maria Szabo in Llandudno it was love at first sight. After courting for a few months, the couple got engaged in January 1943, deciding to marry on 12th June that year.

On the day before his wedding, Whitley, who was stationed on the south coast, was due to travel by train to Llandudno. First thing in the morning, he made an appointment to see doctor Major Abraham Cockcroft-Barker of the Royal Army Medical Corps. Whitley initially consulted the doctor for a problem with his right ear, which turned out to be impetigo. However, he also mentioned that he was supposed to be getting married the next morning and was worried that he might have caught 'a certain disease.'

The doctor took a blood sample to test for venereal disease and advised Whitley to postpone his wedding for a few days until he received the result. Whitley sent a telegram to Maria reading *'Am detained in Military Hospital Preston STOP Cancel everything STOP.'*

Meanwhile, Whitley caught the train to Llandudno as planned. Fellow passenger Hugh Edwards watched him leaning out of the window of the carriage door for some time. Then, near to Chester, as a train approached in the opposite direction, he saw Whitely open the door and leap into its path. The driver of the approaching train had no chance to react and Whitley was killed instantly.

Chester coroner David Hughes held an inquest, at which it was revealed that Whitley's blood test for venereal disease had proved negative. The inquest jury returned a verdict of 'suicide while the balance of his mind was disturbed.' The coroner concluded the inquest, saying 'Although he had nothing to be ashamed of, I feel satisfied he was in an impossible dilemma and I tender my sympathies to all concerned.'

Liverpool, Lancashire

After a four-and-a-half-year engagement to Douglas Stewart Callie, Marjorie Massey of Huskisson Street, Liverpool, was eagerly looking forward to her wedding day on 20th September 1924.

The only fly in the ointment was Marjorie's mother, fifty-one-year-old Margaret Alice Massey. Mrs Massey was absolutely dead set against her daughter's marriage, solely because the newlyweds were planning to take rented rooms in a flat and Mrs Massey felt it would be too degrading for her daughter to live in rooms.

Mrs Massey refused to have anything to do with the wedding plans, leaving the room whenever it was mentioned. Indeed, she even went as far as to consult a priest, who told her that it wasn't possible to stop the marriage on such tenuous grounds. Mrs Massey pleaded with her daughter but Marjorie refused to alter her plans.

In the early hours of the morning of the wedding, Margaret Massey committed suicide by drinking oxalic acid. It is not known whether she intended to actually kill herself or if she just planned to make herself ill, forcing the abandonment of the nuptials. The news was broken to Marjorie by her father, who himself had no objections to the wedding.

Marjorie Massey went ahead with her wedding, later telling the coroner that it was the first time in her life she had ever disobeyed her mother. The inquest returned a verdict of suicide during temporary insanity on Mrs Massey.

Note: Some publications give the wedding date as 31st August 1924.

Wallasey, Lancashire

On 1st September 1922, Marjorie Brakell and James Wilkie married at St Mary's Church Liscard, Wallasey, by Reverend E. Bartlett.

Bartlett was invited to attend the wedding reception at a public hall in Wallasey and later became one of forty out of the eighty guests to be stricken with severe food poisoning. At first, the lobster sandwiches served at the reception were blamed for the outbreak but it emerged that several of those guests who were ill had not eaten them. Copies of the menu were therefore circulated to all the guests, who were asked to cross off any foodstuffs that they didn't eat, in the hope of finding a common denominator amongst those who were ill. (One contemporary newspaper reported that only tee-totallers were affected!)

The symptoms experienced – sickness, diarrhoea, shivering, headache, stomach cramps and rigidity of the limbs – seemed very similar to those experienced by sufferers of arsenical poisoning and it was theorised that the green paint in the newly decorated kitchen could have exuded arsenical vapour, which was subsequently absorbed by the food. This theory was strengthened by the fact that several of the waiting staff at the reception complained of headaches and in addition, the hall keeper and his son, who did not eat any food, were both taken ill immediately before the wedding.

Samples of the food were sent to Dr Beattie of Liverpool University for analysis and he was finally able to lay all theories of arsenical poisoning to rest, having found large numbers of bacilli in an uneaten cream trifle.

Church, near Accrington, Lancashire

On the afternoon of his wedding on 31st October 1903, Patrick Morley and his new brother-in-law, Michael Horan, got into an argument about some furniture in the course of which Horan was stabbed above his right eye with a penknife and fell to the floor. Patrick shouted 'We have got him down and now we'll kill him,', at which his brother, James, piled into the fray, both men punching and kicking Horan as he lay defenceless.

Someone pulled the two brothers off Horan, who immediately fled the house in Church, near Accrington, where the wedding breakfast was being held. Peace reigned for only a few minutes before Patrick accused James of kissing the bride.

Both brothers stripped off their coats and squared up for a fight in the street outside. By this time, Horan had fetched the police and as Constables Sinclair and McCulloch arrived, they suddenly found themselves in the middle of an affray. Both policemen were cut on their face, before the Morley brothers retreated back into the house and barricaded themselves in.

'If any 'bobbies' come in, we'll kill you' they threatened.

The two injured policemen sent for reinforcements and eventually Police Sergeant Thomas and P.C.s Naylor, Greenhalgh, Eastham and Clements managed to force their way into the house and overpower the Morleys.

Both brothers were charged with 'wounding with intent to do grievous bodily harm' and magistrates forwarded their case to the Lancashire Assizes. Both initially pleaded not guilty but midway through the trial, their defence counsel Mr Madden stated that the defendants would be prepared to plead guilty to a lesser charge of 'unlawful wounding. This being acceptable to the prosecution, Madden told the court that the Morley brothers were hard-working men of good character. 'What was done, was done in drink' stated Madden, before pointing out that only Patrick Morley was alleged to have used a knife.

The judge, Mr Justice Ridley, took this into account when sentencing Patrick to eighteen months' imprisonment and James to twelve months.

Kendal, Cumberland

After their wedding reception at St John's Mission Hall, Kendal, on 21st July 1951 Thomas and Leila Nicholson (nee Wood) left for their honeymoon totally unaware that their guests were gradually beginning to feel unwell. In all, fifty of the seventy-eight guests at the reception succumbed to food poisoning, most being treated at the local hospitals.

Medical Officer Dr Frank Madge sent off multiple samples of the foods eaten at the wedding for analysis, including boiled ham and tongue, tinned strawberries, ice cream and wedding cake. Bacteria that might have caused the violent sickness and diarrhoea was found in the tongue, ham and the wedding cake icing.

By coincidence, there were a further twenty-one cases of food poisoning in the area that day, all affecting people who had not attended the wedding. The cause was later determined to be a batch of jellied veal.

Prestwich, Lancashire

On 22nd January 1934, forty-year-old tailoress Eunice Mills and her fiancé Frederick Fairhurst exchanged contracts on a house at Prestwich, which they intended to be their marital home. Completion was scheduled for 12th February but on 1st February a distraught Miss Mills visited the solicitor's office on her own.

She told the solicitor that she had discovered that Frederick didn't live at the address he had given her, which was Sparth Road in Newton Heath and asked if the solicitor had any information that might help her to find him. The solicitor only had the Sparth Road address, which Fairhurst had used when signing the contract to buy the house.

Eunice began searching for Fairhurst, writing to a Mr Fairhurst of Gazell Street, Newton Heath, whose address she found in the telephone directory. She wrote two letters, the first of which read in part *'Dear Fred, I am taking great liberties in writing to you but I have got your address from the directory. I expected to hear from you and I am disappointed.'*

Eunice received no response to either of her letters and, on 2nd February, the day before she and Fairhurst should have married, she was found gassed in the Prestwich house.

Coroner Mr R. Stuart-Rodger opened an inquest on her death. The police had found a small scrap of paper with the Gazell Street address written on it in her handbag. They went to visit the occupier and found that his name was Mr F. Fairhurst but that he wasn't the man who had been courting Eunice. He was castigated by the coroner for opening and keeping the letters, even though they were obviously not intended for his eyes.

It emerged that, in the days before her death, Eunice Mills had made two withdrawals from her bank, one of £30 and the other £20. She had also telephoned the bank authorising her fiancé to withdraw money from her account and he had taken a sum of £33 7s. None of this money was ever recovered.

The coroner then adjourned the inquest indefinitely to allow the police time to find the elusive Frederick Fairhurst.

A photograph of Fairhurst was circulated in the contemporary newspapers and several people came forward with the name Frederick Lee, a married man who lived in Newton Heath. Police discovered that he had married a lady named Miss Maddock in 1923 and they had three children. In 1930, she divorced him and her father was so keen to get rid of Lee that he paid for his passage to Canada. Lee however had other ideas and came home on the next available ship. Within two months, he had married again, siring a further two children. He had numerous affairs during both of his marriages and one of the men who recognised his photograph and communicated his identity to the police was Reverend W. Gower-Jones, who described Lee as '...the most dangerous and plausible liar and scoundrel I have ever come across in my thirty-two years of ministry.'

Lee, an unemployed carpenter, had lived at home with his wife and children until 31st January, when he disappeared.

Brought before the resumed inquest on 20th March 1934, Lee was heavily censured by the coroner, who told him: 'You are a professional seducer and trafficker in souls and bodies of women. Your whole life seems to have been one of adultery. You have caused the death of this woman Eunice Mills by your deception and the law has no power over you...what about the innocent children you have begotten and left to the mercies of the world? There is only one treatment for such as you – the lash and sterilisation. You seem to have brought hell into the lives of many women. Unless you repent, your ultimate destination will be where the worm dieth not and the fire is not quenched.' Stuart-Rodger then told Lee to leave the inquest and get out of his sight.

Finally, the coroner assured Eunice Mill's mother that the inquest jury's verdict of 'suicide while of unsound mind' was no slur on her daughter's mental state.

Birkenhead, Lancashire

Thomas Powell and Elizabeth Lee had been courting for sixteen months and engaged for six of those. Their wedding was arranged for half-past ten on the morning of 13th January 1886 and at nine o'clock, Elizabeth called round to Thomas's lodgings so that the couple could go to the church together.

Thomas was suffering from a heavy cold and, at his suggestion, the couple went into the Stork Hotel on Price Street, where he drank a glass of milk and rum. Thomas told Elizabeth that he had left his wallet at his lodgings, asking her to wait at the hotel for him while he ran back to fetch it. He never came back.

Thomas worked as a cabdriver for the Birkenhead and District Omnibus and Carriage Company and at just before six o'clock on the morning after what should have been his wedding day, he was found hanging in the company's stables at Woodside Ferry.

An inquest on his death was held later that day at the Victoria Hotel in Cleveland Street, where coroner Mr H. Churton gently questioned Elizabeth about her relationship with her fiancé. She told the inquest that he was always kind and affectionate towards her and that she had never heard him say anything to indicate that he might be contemplating suicide. She insisted that he was a sober, steady young man, who had appeared to be eagerly anticipating married life.

Thomas Devine, a fellow cabdriver, stated that he had seen the deceased at the company stables shortly after midnight on Tuesday. Devine wasn't aware that Powell should have married that morning. According to Devine, Powell seemed as normal - he was perfectly sober, but claimed to have misplaced the key to his lodgings. He asked Devine if he might borrow the key to the stables, adding that he intended to bed down there for the night. Devine handed him the key and also gave him a match to light his pipe before bidding him goodnight and leaving.

The following morning, another driver tried unsuccessfully to get into the stables at 5.45 am. Eventually, with some difficulty, John Perkins managed to push the door open, finding that a broom handle had been wedged against it from inside, preventing it from opening normally. On entering the stables, he found Powell hanging from a ladder to a hay loft by a running noose. The body was stiff and cold. In one of Powell's pockets was a note giving the name and address of his father in Wolverhampton.

The coroner commented that this seemed like a most extraordinary case of suicide and one of the most unaccountable and cruel cases in his long experience of such matters. It seemed as though Powell had deliberately set out to be cruel to his fiancée. He had evidently made up his mind to commit suicide but there was little to show the state of his mind at the time. He was obviously not suffering from temporary insanity, nor from the effects of drink. He had seemed perfectly sensible from the moment he left Elizabeth in the pub to his last goodnight with Thomas Devine.

The inquest jury returned the verdict that the deceased committed suicide, adding that there was insufficient evidence to show the state of his mind at the time.

Radcliffe, Manchester

On 8th February 1892, talented Manchester artist Arnold Henry Warden and Miss Alice Heywood were married at the Church of St John the Evangelist, afterwards holding a reception at the bride's father's house.

Warden seemed in high spirits during the reception, laughing and singing and smiling appreciatively at the congratulations and well wishes from the wedding guests. However, shortly after ten o'clock at night, after bidding his new sister-in-law Elizabeth Heywood 'Goodnight', he retired to the drawing room alone. Seconds later, a shot rang out.

People rushed into the drawing room to find Warden lying partly on his back across a table, a six-chambered revolver by his side. It was obvious that he had held the revolver to the side of his head and then pulled the trigger, since the bullet had entered one temple and exited through the other. A doctor was summoned but Warden was beyond medical assistance and died the following morning, having neither moved nor spoken.

Coroner Mr S.F. Butcher held an inquest on 10th February. Warden's father, Henry Forrester Warden, told the coroner that twenty-four-year-old Arnold was his oldest son. He was usually a very cheerful young man but could be rather impulsive at times. Mr Warden had never known his son to carry a gun

During the previous summer, Arnold had fallen down some steps at the home of a friend, since when he had suffered from violent headaches. He was not a drinker and was certainly not under the influence of alcohol at the time of his death, although Elizabeth Heywood did comment that he looked a little blank and strange when he bade her 'Goodnight'.

The inquest jury returned a verdict that Warden shot himself while insane. On 18th July 1892 Alice gave birth to a son, who she named Arnold Henry Forester Warden. Like his father, Warden junior was a talented artist and went on to become a noted illustrator of books and comics.

Whitehaven, Cumberland

Immediately after her marriage to commercial traveller Frederick Dyall on 3rd December 1934, his wife Sarah (nee Benson) was arrested and charged with the theft of £14 from a bedroom at The Grand Hotel, where she worked as a waitress.

Twenty-nine-year-old Sarah pleaded guilty and was bound over and discharged, having promised to pay the money back. Her new husband agreed to stand as security.

Liverpool, Lancashire

On 22nd November 1902, thirty-three-year-old deck labourer Archibald Murphy just happened to bump into a sailor named James Doran on the streets of Liverpool. Doran told Murphy that he had been married that very day and invited him to join in the celebrations.

Murphy willingly went with the sailor to a house in Saltney Street, where there was a lot of drink being consumed in what the contemporary newspapers later described as '…a general orgie' (sic).

Murphy was only too happy to join in but after a spell of singing, dancing, playing the accordion and heavy drinking, he suddenly lay down on the floor and went to sleep. The carousing went on around him until the early hours of the morning, when some of the wedding guests decided it would be charitable to carry him home. It was only on reaching his mother's house and banging on the door for admittance that they realised that Murphy was in fact stone dead.

A post-mortem examination revealed a fractured skull but there was nothing to suggest how or even when the injury was caused. The inquest jury eventually returned an open verdict, the coroner remarking that it was truly disgraceful and shocking that a young couple should commence their married life with an orgy of the character described.

Stanley, Lancashire

On 17th September 1909, twenty-year-old Annie Mabel Collins left her father's Liscard house in the morning. She returned later that afternoon with a man, who she introduced to her father as James Muir Mackridge, claiming they had been married earlier that day.

William Creswell Collins was initially very shocked and told his daughter she was a 'silly girl', at which Annie told him that she had been worried that he would oppose the wedding. However, the marriage was obviously a done deed and, once he had recovered himself, Collins congratulated his daughter, shook his new son-in-law's hand and wished them every happiness.

The newlyweds spent the following evening with Mr Collins and arranged to visit his house for tea on 21st September. However, although Mr Mackridge duly arrived at the appointed time, there was no sign of his wife.

Earlier that morning, Annie had gone to Stanley Station, where a porter had seen her standing on the platform and assumed that she was waiting to meet a friend. Soon afterwards, he heard a train whistle and, when he looked around, he saw she was now kneeling on the railway line. As the train approached, she deliberately stretched out her arms and lay across the line, the train passing straight over her and killing her instantly. When he appeared at the later inquest, the driver of the train stated that he had seen her earlier that day, standing on the edge of the platform of a different station, although she had stepped back when he had sounded his whistle.

Mr Collins told the inquest that his daughter was healthy and had a sunny, cheerful disposition and that his impressions of her new husband were favourable – he saw him as a straightforward and honourable man. Notwithstanding the fact that she had married on impulse and then knelt in front of a train days later, Collins surprisingly told the inquest that his daughter was not normally given to impulsive acts.

Mackridge revealed that he had known his wife for four or five years before their wedding, during which he had asked numerous times if he might meet her parents. The secret wedding had been her idea but she had seemed happy and, when he left to go to work on the morning of his death, she was safe and well at home and showing no signs of having any intention of ending her life.

The inquest returned a verdict of 'suicide during temporary insanity'.

Blackburn, Lancashire

In January 1939, twenty-eight-year-old Joseph Wood fell from a high mill chimney in Blackburn and was fatally injured. His work mate, Clarence Scott, miraculously escaped the same fate by clinging desperately to scaffolding until he was rescued.

Scott and Wood were firm friends and since Joseph had left a widow with two young children, Clarence pledged to look after them. In time, their friendship deepened to a romance and arrangements were made for their marriage on 11 May 1940. However, shortly before their wedding, Clarence fell a distance of 225 feet from the chimney of the Imperial Spinning Mill in Blackburn and was killed.

Imperial Mill, Blackburn, with chimney (author's collection)

'Clarence was an old friend of my late husband and they were together when Joe had his fall. Clarence had a miraculous escape. That he should now have a similar end is tragic in the extreme' stated bereaved bride-to-be Bertha Wood.

Carlisle, Cumberland

On 19th August 1886, John R. Lawson married Rebecca Hodgkinson and after the ceremony, they had a wedding breakfast at the home of the bridegroom's aunt in Spencer Street, Carlisle. No expense was spared for the catering and the aunt hired highly respected cook, Mrs Dunglinson to prepare the feast, as well as another local woman, Mrs Little, to act as a waitress.

The celebrations went very well and, in due course, the newlyweds left for their honeymoon in Edinburgh. However, while visiting an exhibition later that day, both bride and groom began to feel unwell and returned to their hotel. When they were no better two days later, Edinburgh doctor Dr Carmichael was called to attend the couple, particularly Mrs Lawson, who was by then very ill indeed. Carmichael suspected that they had ingested some form of poison, although no trace of anything untoward was found in Mrs Lawson's vomit. Both bride and groom suspected that the game pie served at their wedding reception had been 'a bit off' and put that down to the cause of their illness.

Sadly, Rebecca Lawson's condition gradually worsened and she died on 23rd August. Unbeknown to the newlyweds, back in Carlisle, many of their wedding guests were displaying similar symptoms. They were treated by doctors, including Dr Barnes, who immediately began to try and compile a list of who had eaten what at the reception.

Although Mr and Mrs Lawson had blamed the game pie for their illness, three of those suffering the same symptoms had not eaten any. Of those people who were ill, three had not eaten salmon, three had not eaten wedding cake and only one had not eaten jelly. In conjunction with the Chief Constable of Cumbria, Barnes sent off various items to the Carlisle City Analyst Dr Walker. These included wedding cake, hare soup, cornflour, tea, liquid cochineal, mace and two bottles of vomit from different victims.

Walker analysed all of the items thoroughly, finding no trace whatsoever of any animal or vegetable poison in any of them. To further his tests, he also fed portions of the items he tested to rabbits and mice, who suffered no ill effects at all.

Various theories were put forward as being possible causes for the outbreak of poisoning. It was suggested that some of the food might have been cooked in copper pans but no copper pans at all were used in the preparation of the meal. It was also pointed out that tinned fruit had caused similar outbreaks in the past, but no tinned fruit had been served.

Matters were further complicated when an agency nurse, brought in to care for some of the victims, also went down with similar symptoms. Mrs Clubbs, who had not attended the wedding, was engaged to nurse Mrs Lawson senior and her servant, Jane Turnbull. Mrs Clubbs told doctors that she had eaten very little food while in the house, apart from tea, brown and white breads and a very small piece of ham left over from the wedding.   Accordingly, ham and flour were sent to Walker for analysis.

Perhaps unsurprisingly, since it had been almost a month since the ham was cooked, Walker found that it contained numerous bacilli, which he tried to grow on a variety of mediums. He was unsuccessful and therefore concluded that the bacilli were dead and were not a consequence of putrefaction. Walker fed extracts of the ham to mice, cats, flies and rabbits but once again, none of the animals showed any ill effects.

There was no real official enquiry into the poisoning. Cumberland County Coroner Mr Carrick declined to hold an inquest, as the only victim who had died, had done so in Edinburgh, which was out of his jurisdiction. The ham was one of a consignment of forty-five that had been shipped from America to Liverpool. Most of the other hams in the shipment had been sold to retailers who had then carved small quantities for their customers. Nobody else had suffered any ill effects as a result of consuming the American ham.

In 1887, Dr Barnes gave a lecture on the subject of Food Poisons to the Carlisle Microscopical Society. He touched on the Carlisle wedding poisonings, stating that the ham was the most likely culprit although adding that it had been glazed with gelatine, which was also used for the jellies at the feast. Any gelatinous substance would be a suitable medium for the development and multiplication of harmful organisms, Barnes explained. Since bacilli responsible are normally killed by cooking, he stressed the importance of storing food in dry, well-ventilated conditions.

Coincidentally, there was another mass outbreak of food poisoning in Carlisle in January 1887. This time the cause was narrowed down to pease-pudding and the washing soda that had been used in the cooking process to soften the peas.

Bolton, Lancashire

On Saturday 15th September 1928, twenty-nine-year-old Gertrude Gladys Dyson waited for her groom at Christ Church, Bradford. When he didn't arrive, the vicar had no option other than to tell Gertrude and the fifty wedding guests that the wedding was off.

The distraught bride was taken to her brother's house in a state of collapse. Meanwhile, several of the guests went to Clayton Labour Club and went ahead with the meal planned for the reception.

Sam Beaumont had known Gertrude for three years and the couple had been engaged for a year. According to his father, he had left the house earlier that morning intending to visit the bath house but had not returned.

Nothing was heard of Beaumont until the Monday after the planned wedding when cleaner Mrs Dickisnon let herself into the offices of the London and North East Railway in Bolton, where he had worked as a clerk for the past fifteen years and was a much-valued employee. She found him lying on the floor, with a cushion under his head. One end of a rubber tube was in his mouth, the other end being connected to a gas stove. In one of his pockets was a note reading *'My dear father and mother, please forgive me but my poor brain has gone. Your broken -hearted son, Sam.'*

At an inquest held on 19th September, the jury were told that Gertrude's brother Arthur, who was to act as best man, had seen Beaumont the evening before the wedding. Sam was then a little quiet but apparently this was not unusual as he was suffering from a severe ear infection in his left ear, which caused him chronic pain and made him partially deaf.

The coroner ruled that Beaumont had committed suicide while suffering from a temporarily unsound mind.

Note: Some accounts state that Gertrude had not actually gone to the church but was waiting at her brother's house, intending to leave once she was told that the groom had arrived.

Preston, Lancashire

John Simpson and Annie Ratcliffe (courtesy of Preston Digital Archives)

Sixteen-year-old Annie Ratcliffe was the daughter of Alfred Ratcliffe, the licensee of the Blue Bell Inn, on Church Street, Preston. One of Alfred's more regular customers was twenty-one-year-old

John 'Jack' Aspinall Simpson, a well-educated man who usually worked as a clerk but had recently 'given way to drink' and was without a job. Annie was so infatuated with him that she frequently stole small amounts of money from her father to give to Simpson

Annie's father was horrified by his daughter's attraction to Simpson and did everything he possibly could to separate the two young people, including banning Simpson from the pub. However, the couple continued to meet in secret and Annie became pregnant. In despair, she wrote to Simpson:

'Dear Jack, I think you had better come down either tonight or in the morning and ask him what he has against you and I speaking. If I have not to speak to you again, I have made up my mind to do away with myself, as I cannot live without seeing or speaking to you. I am nearly heart-broken. Good-bye for the present. A million kisses from your darling wife A. SIMPSON (sic). Excuse bad writing and spelling. Written in haste. Tell him that you really love me and if he will only serve you, you will wait a few years for me.'

Simpson, who had once worked for the local registrar, managed to procure a consent form, which had to be signed by Annie's father, since she was only sixteen years old. Having initially refused to sign, Alfred eventually relented, probably because of his daughter's pregnancy.

Simpson told Annie that he had made arrangements for them to be married on 2nd August 1881 but the couple were seen in a pub that day, Annie sobbing bitterly. When her sister Edith confronted Simpson, he explained that it wasn't convenient for the registrar to marry them that day, adding that he had organised a wedding at St Paul's Church for the following day.

On 3rd August, Annie dressed in her wedding dress and went to meet her fiancé. The two of them went into The Walter Scott Inn, where they went into the parlour having purchased two small bottles of lemonade. They had been there a few minutes when the daughter of landlady Ann Quigley heard a strange noise. On investigation, she found Annie staggering towards the door, blood pouring from her throat and soaking her wedding dress.

The Walter Scott Inn, Preston (courtesy of Preston Digital Archives)

Miss Quigley called out to her mother, who attracted the attention of a man named Bernard McGuire who happened to be walking past the pub. When McGuire went into the parlour, he found Annie Ratcliffe lying on the floor in a pool of blood, a bloody razor beside her. Simpson sat calmly at a table, one hand in his pocket, the other on his knee.

'Who has done this?' McGuire asked him.

'I did' replied Simpson, adding that he didn't know why he had done it.

The police were sent for and Simpson was taken to the police station, while Annie's corpse was conveyed to the mortuary, where it was found that her head had been almost severed from her body. Meanwhile, Simpson's two sisters were waiting at home dressed in their wedding outfits, intending to accompany the couple to the church for the ceremony.

At an inquest held at the Police Station by coroner Mr W. Gilbertson, the jury needed less than two minutes deliberation to find a verdict of wilful murder against Simpson, who was committed for trial at the next Manchester Assizes.

His trial took place on 7th November 1881 before Mr Justice Kay. There it emerged that a mutual friend of Annie and Simpson had asked him 'Why don't you get married? You have courted long enough.'

Simpson's response was apparently 'To hell with getting married. I am only after the cash bags there.'

Found guilty of wilful murder, Simpson was sent to Strangeways Prison, where he apparently became a reformed character in the run up to his execution. He wrote to a friend *'Yes, it is bad company that has ruined me and if I had taken the advice of my mother, I should have been a deal different. I am happy to tell you that I go to church every day and twice on Sundays and that I read my Bible every day. Thank God I can say from my heart that I am truly sorry for all my sins.'* He kept a photograph of Annie in his cell and requested that it should be buried with him after his execution.

Before his death, Simpson sent word to Albert Ratcliffe, asking to see him. Ratcliffe refused, but did send a message of forgiveness, from which Simpson took great comfort.

On the 28th November 1891, the day of his execution, he walked calmly to his appointment with executioner William Marwood. However, things did not go according to plan and Simpson was seen to struggle on the noose for almost a minute. A later post mortem examination showed that he died from strangulation rather than the severance of his spinal cord.

Note: Some accounts give Simpson's age as twenty-three, not twenty-one.

Near Penwortham, Lancashire

On the morning of Saturday 15th September 1866, John Turner and Mary Elizabeth Ingham were married at St James's Church in Accrington, Lancashire. The other members of the bridal party were Elizabeth and Mary Ellen Aspden, Robert Chippendale and John Rawcliffe, who were all weavers.

The party intended to spend the weekend in nearby Preston and, on the afternoon of the wedding, they hired a boat from Hesketh's Boat House. Chippendale, Mary Ellen and the newlyweds got into the boat, the other couple intending to follow the boat on foot on the riverbank.

'We will have you in the river before we get back' joked the men as they set off to row. They got as far as Ribblesplace before the prediction came true. As the oarsmen were turning the boat for the return journey it overturned. Turner, Chippendale and Mary Ellen managed to grab hold of the boat and clung to it as it drifted towards the Penwortham side of the river but nineteen-year-old Mary was swept away by the current.

Her body was snagged by angler John Irving the following day. She was much disfigured and her bonnet and shawl were missing.

Coroner Mr Myres held an inquest at the Fleece Inn, at which the jury heard that while Turner was an experienced rower, Chippendale was less so and kept missing his stroke. Eventually, the boat turned sideways and began to fill with water before overturning.

The inquest jury seemed to find Chippendale's inexperience as an oarsman to have been a major factor in Mary's death, although they fell short of saying so directly, finding that Mary Turner was accidentally drowned by the upsetting of a boat.

Darcy Lever, near Bolton, Lancashire

On 23rd March 1882, thirty-five-year-old collier Peter Heyes and weaver Nancy Entwistle were married at the Wesleyan Chapel in Darcy Lever, near Bolton. After the ceremony, they went to their marital home in Radcliffe Road, Darcy Lever, which had previously belonged to the bride's mother.

On the following day, Heyes suggested to his new wife that they should go for a walk together. She agreed and he went upstairs to get ready. Moments later, Mrs Heyes heard a thud and, on running upstairs to see what had made the noise, she was horrified to find her husband kneeling down on their bedroom floor, his throat cut and a bloody razor by his side. Having severed both his windpipe and his gullet, he was beyond medical help and died within the hour.

At an inquest on Heyes's death, Nancy told the coroner that Heyes was a widower, who had two young children by his first marriage. He had begun courting her shortly after his first wife's death three months earlier and had quickly proposed marriage.

However, about a fortnight before the wedding, his demeanour changed dramatically. He asked Nancy to postpone the wedding, saying that his mother-in-law had objected, believing that he was marrying too soon after his first wife's death. Nancy had already given notice to her landlord and arranged her house move and so refused to allow the ceremony to be delayed. Heyes had apparently accepted her decision with good grace and the wedding went ahead as planned. There had been no quarrel between the newlyweds and Nancy couldn't think of a single reason why her husband might have killed himself.

The inquest returned a verdict of 'suicide whilst in a state of temporary insanity'.

Bolton, Lancashire

Twenty-one-year-old Louisa Thurlby (or Thorlby) had been courting twenty-two-year-old carter George Brown for some years. Their wedding was arranged for the first week in June 1896 and, on the evening of 28th May, the couple went out to buy a wedding ring.

Deansgate, Bolton (author's collection)

Louisa was working as a waitress in a restaurant in Deansgate, Bolton, and living over the premises. When Brown escorted her home that evening, the couple seemed on the best of terms. When Louisa went upstairs to her bedroom, Brown followed her and a few moments later, her landlord heard her screaming desperately. He rushed upstairs, meeting Louisa on the landing, bleeding from a terrible gash in her throat. 'George has done this' she proclaimed, before collapsing.

The police were called and Louisa was sent to hospital, where she underwent an operation. Everyone had been so preoccupied with helping her that little thought had been given to George, who the police found in Louisa's bedroom, his throat so badly cut with a razor that his head was almost severed from his body.

It was obvious that George had planned to kill his fiancée, since he didn't normally use a razor and had bought one specially to murder. At the inquest on his death, the coroner suggested a verdict of *felo de se* but the jury disagreed, deciding that Brown had been temporarily insane when he attempted to murder Louisa then killed himself.

Northern Ireland

Magheraleave, near Lisburn

Mary Ann Lowry lived on a 4½ acre farm at Magheraleave, in the parish of Derriaghy, near Lisburn. The farm had belonged to her father, Henry, who died on 29th April 1905. Lowry left a will stating that, on his death, the farm should be left outright to Mary Ann for the period of her lifetime. On her death, the property would be equally divided between her two younger brothers, James and Thomas.

The two young men both lived and worked on the farm, paying rent to their sister, James twenty shillings a week and Thomas sixteen. The arrangement worked well until Mary Ann, who was already in her late forties, began courting James Potts and told her brothers that she was planning to marry.

James and Thomas were adamant that they would not allow another man into the house, husband or no husband. Hence, on 3rd July 1924, Mary Ann married and returned to the farm alone, her brothers having threatened to do Potts an injury if he returned with her. They believed that she should leave the farm to them and go to her new husband's home in Lisburn if she wanted to live with him as man and wife.

The newlyweds continued to live apart until it was suggested that Mary Ann sued her brothers for trespass. She took a test case before the local magistrates, accusing them of trespass on 1st, 2nd and 3rd September 1924 and of refusing to leave her home when asked to do so. The magistrates found in her favour, fining Thomas and James 2s and 6d plus costs each, with seven days in Belfast Gaol if they defaulted on payment.

Her brothers appealed the judgement and it was eventually referred to the King's Bench Division of the Northern High Court.

It was argued that the brothers had no legal rights to live in the property other than as their sister's lodgers. Counsel for the Lowry brothers maintained that they were more than just lodgers, having lived and worked on the farm for more than twenty years, contributing to its upkeep and development. Nevertheless, the higher court upheld the magistrates' decision and Mary Ann was at last able to live in her own home as a married woman.

Dungiven, County Derry

In certain parts of rural Ireland, it was the custom to fire shots over the heads of the wedding party for the purpose of saluting the happy couple and wishing them well. Hence, on 27th December 1906, when James McCloskey saw a car with bridesmaids on their way to the bride's house before proceeding to the Roman Catholic Church at Dungiven for the wedding, he hurried into a nearby house and asked to borrow a gun.

He loaded it with powder and, as the bridesmaids passed, he fired his salute. To his horror, the gun was already loaded with pellets and bridesmaid Cassie Gilderson took the shot full in the face from a range of four or five yards. Part of her neck was blown clean away, her jugular vein was severed and one of her eyes was completely destroyed.

Cassie was fully expected to die and McCloskey was swiftly arrested and charged with wounding, but was released on bail.

He appeared at the Dungiven Petty Sessions no less than four times, the magistrates adjourning the case every time in the hope that Cassie might recover sufficiently to give evidence. Eventually, on his fifth appearance in May 1907, Cassie was present in court, still very weak and frail, her face terribly disfigured.

Nevertheless, the first thing that Cassie said to the magistrates was that she realised that the shooting had been nothing more than a terrible accident and she hoped that they would clear McCloskey.

McCloskey and another witness swore that they had both checked the gun before charging it with powder and both believed it to be unloaded. It was argued in court that the shooting was meant to be a gesture of goodwill and friendship and, unable to show any evidence of malice or intent to injure, magistrates voted unanimously to acquit McCloskey, although they stated that they hoped that lessons would be learned from his experience.

Downpatrick, County Down

On 11th October 1845, Robert Beadnell married Annie Bright in Tullyish Church. Sadly, Annie died from a fever the following year but on 15th December 1846, her widow married for a second time – to his mother-in-law, Sarah Ann Bright.

There were understandably some doubts as to the legality of the marriage, with particular regard to the degree of affinity between them. In Roman Catholic law, affinity due to a relationship created by a previous marriage is seen as an impediment to the marriage of any couple and those who enter into such a relationship are regarded as incestuous. Since both Robert and Sarah had told the registrar that there was no just cause or impediment to their marriage, it was decided that both should be tried for perjury and they were brought before Chief Barron Piggott at the County Down Summer Assizes.

The counsel for their defence, Mr Ross Moore, argued that before the couple could be convicted of perjury, two facts must be established; the first being that the couple were aware that their intended marriage fell within the prohibited degree of affinity and the second that the prohibition of degrees of affinity formed part of the laws of the land.

For the Crown, Sir Thomas Staples argued that the degrees of affinity were part and parcel of the laws of the land and should therefore be known to every citizen. It could scarcely be believed that any man was so ignorant that he did not know that he was not at liberty to marry the mother of his own wife. However, the relevant Act of Parliament banning such marriages appeared to apply solely to

England, rather than Northern Ireland. The prosecution tried to prove that the defendants were churchgoers, who would have known the degrees of affinity from their prayer book, but neither of the couple was a regular worshipper. In addition, the prosecution was unable to produce a single statute in which the prohibitions were documented.

Moore let it be known that he strongly objected to the founding of a prosecution on the Book of Common Prayer or an English Act of Parliament, since no similar act had been in force in Ireland at the time of the marriage.

In his address to the jury, Piggott stated that to convict the couple of perjury, it must be proven that they knew that they were taking a false oath and, while there was little doubt that a false oath had been taken, he personally did not believe that it had been done wilfully or corruptly. Even so, the jury debated for three hours before returning to court to say that they were unable to agree on a verdict.

Eventually, the judge discharged the jury and released the prisoners on bail to appear again in court if called upon to do so.

Belfast

Cashier William Mills married collar factory inspector Agnes Bryson at Christchurch, Belfast on 17th January 1912. Shortly after the ceremony, Agnes began to feel unwell and a doctor was called to attend to her.

He diagnosed appendicitis and sadly the bride died shortly before midnight on her wedding day. Thus, Mills went from being a bachelor, to a bridegroom, to a husband, to a widower in a matter of hours.

Knocknamuckley Church, near Portadown, County Armagh

Interior of Knocknamuckley Church (author's collection)

Elizabeth 'Lizzie' McGreedy's mother was a sexton at Knocknamuckley Church and, on the morning of 2nd March 1888, Elizabeth went to open the church for a wedding that was to take place at ten o'clock. Soon afterwards, Reverend Oates arrived and shortly after him, a man named William Thompson entered the church. William was the brother of the groom's first wife, who had died on 17th March 1887.

William Thompson asked Elizabeth what time the wedding was due to take place and she told him. He then asked if there was anyone else in the church and, when she said that there were only herself and the vicar, he sat down in a pew near the church door.

Knocknamuckley Church (author's collection)

The wedding party of six people arrived, led by groom widower Thomas Thompson and bridesmaid Mary Ann Moffat. They were followed by the bride, Fanny Jane Moffat and the best man, William Coulter, then Joseph Twinam (or Twynam) and Margaret Dilworth brought up the rear. As the groom walked up the aisle towards the altar, William Thompson left his pew and fell into step behind him. There was a sudden loud bang and Thomas shouted 'I've been shot!' As William tried to shoot a second time, Thomas spun round and grabbed hold of the revolver, hanging onto it for dear life until Twinam came to his assistance. With the assistance of coachman William Phoenix, who had driven the party to church, they managed to disarm William and passed the revolver to the vicar, who immediately took it to the vestry and locked it in the safe.

Twinam then hurried to Portadown to fetch the police and a doctor and when Detective Inspector Leatham reached the church,

William approached him saying 'I am the man'. He was arrested but said nothing more.

Thomas Thompson had a bullet wound in his left shoulder, although he was still conscious and managed to make a deposition, naming his brother-in-law, William, as the person who had shot him. Thomas explained that William was the brother of his first wife and that they had not spoken since her death. There was also bad blood between Thomas and his first wife's mother. Medical assistance came promptly, but the injury proved fatal and Thomas died later that evening. A post mortem examination revealed that the single bullet had entered his body about two inches below his left shoulder. It had fractured his ninth rib, passed into the pleural cavity through the base of the left lung then through the diaphragm and spleen and into the upper stomach, lodging just below the left nipple.

Coroner Mr William H. Atkinson held an inquest on the death of Thomas Thompson, at which the jury concluded that he '... died from the effects of a bullet wound inflicted by William Thompson and that the said William Thompson did feloniously and with malice aforethought kill and slay said Thomas Thompson.' The jury further stated that there was insufficient evidence to show whether or not William Thompson was of unsound mind, which the coroner deemed a matter for the Assize judge when the accused stood trial.

While William Thompson was in prison awaiting his trial, police arrested his mother, Elizabeth 'Essie' Thompson, and charged her with having incited her son to murder Thomas. It was alleged that Essie had remarked to William in front of several witnesses that he was no man, or he would have put a bullet into Thomas and, had she been in his shoes, she would have done so long ago. Mrs Thompson was taken before magistrates but while there were a number of witnesses who had heard her remarks, there were also several who swore that she had never made them. Magistrates eventually concluded that there was insufficient evidence to send her for trial at the Assizes and she was discharged.

At William's trial before Mr Justice Murphy on 10 July 1888, it emerged that he had purchased the revolver and bullets the day before the murder. Although there was no real motive suggested, it was stated that William was extremely fond of his sister and fell into a deep depression when she died. In addition, Thomas had a child with his first wife, and William did not believe that Fanny Moffat would be a suitable stepmother to his niece.

Since William had shot his brother-in-law in broad daylight, in front of several witness, his defence counsel, George H. Smith, had a difficult job to try and persuade a jury that he was not guilty as charged. Smith tried to induce them to consider the lesser offence of manslaughter, but this approach was quickly quashed by Mr Justice Murphy. Hence Smith's only option was an insanity defence and since William had displayed no signs of insanity either before or after the murder, other than depression at the loss of his sister, Smith was fighting a losing battle.

The jury needed only twelve minutes' deliberation to find William Thomas guilty of murder and sentence of death was duly passed. Asked if he had anything to say, William readily admitted his guilt and stated that he had never claimed to be insane, saying that he had not been trying to prevent Thomas from marrying again. He talked of a long-standing hatred of Thomas, born from what he believed was his brother-in-law's maltreatment and neglect of his late sister. Thomas and his first wife had been estranged at the time of her death. William alleged that Thomas had been a bad husband, who had accused his wife of unfaithfulness and left William to pay all her medical expenses while she was dying, not even bothering to attend her funeral, which William was forced to pay for. 'Every time his name was mentioned, I could not overcome my feelings', William continued. He told the court that he had desperately wanted to leave the country and his memories but that he had been dissuaded from doing so because of concerns about how it would affect his mother. 'I have broken the law and I deserve to die' he concluded.

The execution was fixed for 8th August but shortly before it was due to take place, the sentence was commuted to one of life imprisonment and William was taken to Mountjoy Prison. He was quickly moved to Dundrum Asylum, Dublin, but allegedly remained there only a few weeks before escaping. In spite of extensive searches, William managed to elude capture until 10th September 1906, when he walked into the police barracks at Markethill and gave himself up.

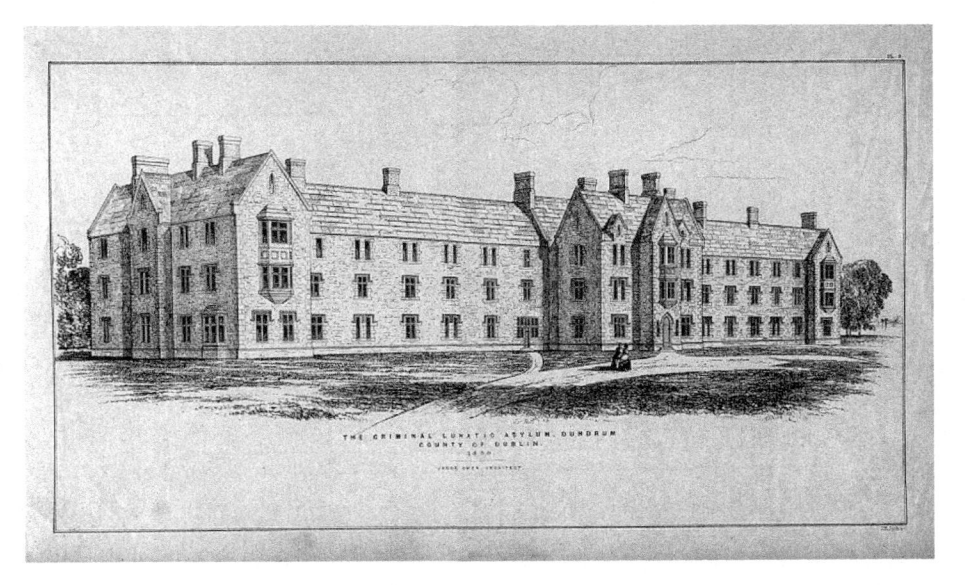

Dundrum Asylum (author's collection)

Reports in the contemporary newspapers seem to indicate that it was likely that Thompson would be returned to Dundrum. However, some sources view William's escape and subsequent recapture as an urban myth. Although there are definitely reports in the contemporary press that he handed himself in, it has proved impossible to verify.

Note: Some newspaper reports name William's mother as Essie Hobson.

Portrush, County Antrim

On 2nd October 1909, thirty-six-year-old Sophia Thompson and her near neighbour, James Hackett, took the train from Portrush to Ballymoney, where they were married by Registrar John Tweed. Immediately after the ceremony, Hackett began celebrating his nuptials, becoming steadily more drunk as the day went on. Eventually, he and Sophia quarrelled about his drinking and travelled back to their respective homes on Causeway Street separately.

Causeway Street, Portrush (author's collection)

Sadly, the couple met up again in Portrush where several witnesses saw and heard Hackett beating his wife. Amidst the sounds of heavy blows and desperate screams, Hackett was heard to ask Sophia 'Is that enough?', to which she replied simply 'You coward'. Unfortunately, 'Big Jim' Hackett had something of a reputation in town and none of the neighbours dared to intervene to assist Sophia.

James returned to his home without his new bride and his concerned sisters went out to look for her. They found her lying by the wall of the Kelly Schools, in a very weakened state. Between them, Annie and Mary Hackett carried Sophia to her own home (55

Causeway Street) and sent for a doctor to attend her. Sadly, when Dr J. C. Martin arrived, Sophia was already dead. The doctor contacted the police, who went to James's house at 59 Causeway Street, finding him fast asleep in bed. He was arrested and charged with the manslaughter of his new wife.

Martin later conducted a post-mortem examination on Sophia. He found no traces of alcohol in her system, nor any marks on her body apart from a few small bruises – what he did find was that she suffered from chronic fatty degeneration of the heart and, even without being beaten, he estimated her life expectancy would have been little more than five years. He recorded the cause of death as being due to syncope, caused by fatty degeneration of the heart but added that her disease was so advanced that any blow or blows would have accelerated her death.

When Hackett appeared in court, magistrates spent over nine hours listening to details of the case before deciding that it should be forwarded to the Ulster Winter Assizes. Hackett pleaded not guilty but, midway through his trial, his defence counsel Thomas Campbell put forward a guilty plea. Campbell told the court that his client was deeply attached to the deceased and bitterly regretted her death, which would never have happened if he hadn't been drunk.

Having given medical evidence earlier in the trial, Dr Martin was recalled to provide a character witness for Hackett, who he described as a man of good character, although inclined to be somewhat broody ad very passionate when drunk.

The judge retired to consider a sentence, eventually deciding that three years' penal servitude was appropriate.

Belfast

On 8th February 1893, Mr Hugh Joseph Davison married Miss Maggie Erwin McMurtry at the Independent Church in Belfast.

The doors to the church were approached by a flight of stone steps and ornamental balustrades and, as the bride and groom were about to leave the church, almost two hundred people piled onto the steps hoping for a better view of the newlyweds. As the crowd surged forwards, the steps and balustrades collapsed. Some people fell and others were showered with chunks of masonry.

Within moments there was, as described in the contemporary newspapers '...a scene of indescribable confusion and panic.' Order was eventually restored by the police, who found that there were actually only four casualties whose injuries were serious enough to merit hospital treatment. Lizzie Percy (16) suffered scalp wounds and contusions to her arm, Sarah Boyle (48) had broken ribs and a head injury, Minnie McKee (25) and Jessie Andrews (28) both had scalp wounds and concussion.

Carrigans, County Donegal

Twenty-four-year-old Lieutenant William George McClintock was riding his horse in a steeplechase at Sandown Park in April 1938 when it fell, crushing him beneath it and leaving him with no feeling or movement below his arms. His mother, Margaret Jennie McClintock, was devastated and told her husband numerous times that both she and her son would be better off dead, suggesting to Colonel Robert Lyle McClintock that the whole family should commit suicide.

Accompanied by his fiancée, twenty-two-year-old Helen Macworth, William was transported back to the family home, Dunmore House, where his mother became his main carer, assisted by two professional nurses. Although his mother strongly disapproved of the union, William's health was deteriorating and he and Helen decided to marry on 26th September 1938, which was his twenty-fifth birthday.

On 24th September, the sun was shining and William asked to be taken out into the garden for some fresh air. He was carried out on a stretcher and was writing a letter to an aunt, when his mother went out into the garden and shot him in the head. Soon afterwards, his body was discovered by his father and he was carried upstairs to his bedroom and laid on the bed.

It was the custom of the house to ring a dinner gong in the hall if Mrs McClintock was wanted and, when she didn't respond, a search was made of the house and grounds. Her body was discovered by a shed in the garden, a shotgun propped between her legs, pointing upwards. (Some reports state that her head was blown clean off her body by the shotgun's blast, coming to rest in a nearby tree.)

Meanwhile, Helen had been informed of her fiancé's death and one of the nurses stayed with her and tried to comfort her. She was absolutely distraught, saying that she couldn't possibly live without William and, when she was finally left alone for a few minutes, she too shot herself, dying from her injuries within the hour.

Coroner Dr S. Kerrigan held an inquest on the three deaths, hearing that fifty-eight-year-old Margaret McClintock had been neurotic, anxious and depressed after her son's accident and had frequently suggested that she and her son would both be better off dead, something her husband had always dismissed as 'just talk'. On several occasions during the past three months, she had been 'raving' but McClintock said he paid little attention to her. She had been involved in a car accident in December 1937 and had suffered a head injury, and Colonel McClintock believed that she was leading up to a nervous breakdown, and her mind had finally snapped on the day of the shootings, believing that she would lose William if she allowed him to marry and that his wife would not be able to take care of him properly.

The inquest found a verdict of murder against Margaret McClintock for her son's death and suicide while of unsound mind in respect of both her death and his fiancée's. Helen was buried on her wedding day, wearing her wedding dress. Her little dog Barney was put to sleep and buried with her.

At the funeral, Reverend David Kelly referred to the tragedies as '...a triumph of love'. He spoke of a mother thinking about her beloved son's future welfare and doing what she believed was best for him, before taking her own life. Miss Macworth had also taken her own life but that too was done in love. 'The bond of love was stronger than the thread of life' intoned Kelly.

After the funerals, Colonel McClintock apparently gave an order that everything belonging to his son and his wife should be burned.

Note: In the contemporary newspaper reports, there is some dispute about whether the location of this tragedy was in Northern Ireland or the Republic of Ireland. It was said to be about six miles to the west of Londonderry, so has been included in Northern Ireland.

Scotland

Dunfermline, Fife

Their wedding was due to take place at the North Parish Church, Dunfermline, on 1st June 1936. However, at the exact moment that he should have been exchanging vows with his bride, bus conductress Janet Anderson, twenty-six -year-old George Clark died in the Dunfermline and West Fife Hospital.

Clark had been admitted to hospital the previous week following a relapse after an attack of pleurisy and was fully expected to survive.

Buckpool, Banffshire

Peter 'Rosie' Reid of the Royal Flying Corps had arranged leave to marry Jeannie Bowie of Buckpool on 18th June 1917. However, less than an hour before the time of the ceremony at the South United Free Church, the bride's family received a telegram from Ireland.

Her two brothers – James and John – had been part of a five-man crew on a small boat engaged in salvaging a steam drifter. The boat had capsized and, although three of the crew were rescued, the two brothers sadly drowned.

The wedding and reception were immediately cancelled but as Rosie's leave expired the following day, the couple elected to get married quietly that evening at her parents' home. Miss Bowie wore black rather than her wedding dress.

Symington, South Lanarkshire

As the train pulled into Symington Station on 30th April 1930, a man was found dead in a third-class carriage. He was sitting in the corner, his head propped up on one arm, a box of flowers and an attaché case on the seat by his side.

The man was placed on a stretcher and taken to Motherwell, where he was searched. No clues to his identity were found apart from a train ticket in his pocket indicating that he had started his journey in Lockerbie and was travelling to Coatbridge.

A message was sent to Coatbridge, where Miss Alison McCallum and her guests were already at the church, waiting for the arrival of her bridegroom. When he didn't turn up, he was reported missing to the police, who quickly realised that they may have found the identity of their mystery corpse. Alison's father, Thomas, and another relative immediately travelled to Motherwell, where they were able to confirm that the deceased was Alison's fiancé, thirty-two-year-old gardener William Simpson.

A post-mortem examination revealed that Simpson had a dislocated larynx as well as signs of a blow on the right-hand side of his forehead. Just three days before his wedding, Simpson had been fumigating a greenhouse, when he bumped into a doorframe and spilled the chemicals he was using. He was immediately overcome with fumes, so much so that he had to crawl out of the greenhouse and was violently sick. He continued to vomit for two days but was determined to be well enough to get married.

It was believed that he had experienced another bout of nausea while travelling to his wedding and had leaned out of the train window, either to vomit or just for some fresh air. It was supposed that he hit his head, perhaps on a passing train or a bridge.

Bo'ness, West Lothian

Bo'ness (author's collection)

John Seddon of Bo'ness had fought on the battlefields of Belgium in the World War before being invalided out of the Army with severe frostbite and returning to his previous job as a miner.

He met Jane Law and the couple began courting. When Jane left Scotland for a position as a domestic servant in England, they continued their courtship by letter and, on Jane's return to Bo'ness, twenty-four-year-old Seddon proposed.

The wedding was arranged for October 1915 and a house was furnished ready for the couple to start their married life. However, Jane was only eighteen years old and, as the wedding date neared, she began to have serious doubts and, after talking to her mother, she decided that she couldn't go through with the marriage.

Her friends Joan Hope and Maggie Vance should have been her bridesmaids and, on the day before the wedding, they were cleaning the house in readiness for the newlyweds when Seddon came and broke the news that there was to be no wedding. Joan had already commented to Maggie earlier that day that she wished it was her who was getting married, so she suggested to John that he should toss a coin and that the winner would take Jane Law's place.

'Heads Miss Hope, tails Miss Vance' Seddon called, as he tossed his lucky farthing. Miss Hope won and, with Miss Vance having agreed to be her bridesmaid, she and Seddon went to see the vicar to ask if Seddon could go through with the wedding arranged for the following day, albeit with a different bride.

After consultation with his bishop, the vicar told Seddon that the banns had been read in Miss Law's name and so he couldn't possibly marry Seddon to a different woman until at least three months had elapsed. Although Joan Hope was happy to wait, as soon as her mother heard of her plans, she forbade the marriage.

However, all was not lost for Seddon. A young woman named Miss Errington read about his plight in the contemporary newspapers and sent him a sympathetic note. This led to what was described in the contemporary newspapers as '...a brief and ardent courtship' between the two, culminating in their marriage at Bo'ness in January 1916.

Colmonell, Ayrshire

On 12th November 1908, Alexander Beattie fell down dead. The fifty-year-old widower was the highly respected head teacher of Colmonell Public School and was due to be married the next morning.

His body was found by his housekeeper, sixty-five-year-old Agnes Ferguson, who collapsed with shock and died a few minutes later.

Glasgow, Lanarkshire

On 12th October 1928, there was a terrible rail crash at Glasgow, which occurred when the Glasgow to Edinburgh passenger train was hit from behind by an engine pulling an empty carriage. More than fifty passengers were seriously injured, and rescuers were hampered both by the location of the accident in a tunnel and by heavy fog. Fortunately, a party of thirty ambulancemen were in training nearby and they rushed to assist.

One man was pulled from the twisted wreckage with severe crush injuries to his legs and abdomen. Although it was fairly obvious that he was beyond any medical assistance, a doctor pulled aside his clothing to check for a heartbeat. As he did, a shower of confetti fell from his clothing and a crushed carnation was seen in his button hole.

The dead man was identified as twenty-five-year-old Mr Donaldson-Gray, who had married his bride Helen Chalmers just three hours earlier. Mrs Gray was taken to hospital, where she lay in a critical condition, one of her legs so badly damaged that it was necessary to amputate it.

When the news of the crash broke and it was reported that a bridegroom had been injured, police were contacted by relatives of another newly-wed couple, who were taken to the mortuary to view Donaldson-Gray's remains. It emerged that James Ross and his new bride, Margaret (nee Nummey) had set off for their honeymoon on the same train. It was established that Mr Ross had been taken to the Western Infirmary and his wife to the Royal Infirmary, where both were suffering from severe leg injuries.

Mr Ross was a widower with a seven-year-old son and only that morning, his landlady had wished him good luck. 'Our married life will just be what luck makes it' Ross replied.

Mr and Mrs Ross and Mrs Gray survived the crash, the primary cause of which was determined to be a signalling error. By a cruel twist of fate, Mr and Mrs Gray almost missed the train after their luggage was accidentally locked in a room at the restaurant where they held their wedding reception. It took ten minutes of frantic searching by the restaurant manageress to locate a spare key to the room and the couple arrived at the station only just in time to board the train. A survivor of the crash later stated that Mr Gray had told him that they had chosen to travel home by train as it was safer than driving on dark nights.

Gress, Isle of Lewis

Malcolm Macleod of Kyles-Scalpay, Isle of Harris was expecting to marry on 21st January 1941. However, as the date of his wedding neared, the area was affected by terrible blizzards, closing the roads and bringing all transport to a halt.

On 18th January, Macleod set out by bus for his fiancée Marion's home at Gress, Isle of Lewis. The bus soon got stuck in a snow drift, forcing Macleod to trudge 10 miles through deep snow to the nearest Post Office, so that he could telegraph his bride and inform her of his predicament. He then set out on foot to walk the fifty miles to Gress.

He walked for a whole day, battling through blizzards and steep snowdrifts until he reached Scaladale, on the borders of Lewis and Harris. There someone took pity on him and let him spend the night at their house, but early the following morning, he set off again.

He had walked nearly half the distance to Gress when a van overtook him and stopped to give him a lift. He arrived at his fiancée's home completely exhausted, half an hour before the wedding was set to take place.

Fortunately, the bride had postponed the ceremony for twenty-four hours and, after a good night's sleep, the wedding went ahead the next day. In all, Merchant Seaman Macleod had walked more than forty miles, on almost impassable roads in the depths of winter.

Edinburgh, Midlothian

ROYAL INFIRMARY OF EDINBURGH

On 2nd August 1929, five men were badly burned in a devastating gas explosion at the Prestonlinks Colliery near Edinburgh. One was twenty-six-year-old John Morton, who had been on the point of marrying his fiancée, twenty-two-year-old Nessie Anderson of Musselburgh.

The banns had already been read and, although badly injured, Morton insisted that the wedding would go ahead. When he realised that he was dying, arrangements were made for the Reverend David Duncan of North Esk to attend his bedside at the Edinburgh Royal Infirmary. Tragically, Morton died on 5th August, just three minutes before the vicar arrived to perform the ceremony.

The disaster went on to claim one more life, that of nineteen-year-old John Byrne. It was later claimed that the explosion was caused by one of the miners striking a match to light a cigarette.

Glasgow, Lanarkshire

On 30th July 1927, Archibald MacGregor (or McGregor) and Annie White of Glasgow got married. Neighbours, Edward and Elizabeth Boyle, were invited to the wedding but Edward was unable to get time off work to attend, so Elizabeth spent the morning helping prepare the wedding breakfast at her neighbour's house in Hartfield Street and then she and her husband attended the celebrations together when he returned home from work.

Elizabeth had been drinking steadily for most of the day and was said to be very drunk. At one stage, she and Edward quarrelled and Elizabeth picked up first a breadknife, then a smoothing iron and threatened her husband with them. She was disarmed by other guests.

The Boyles had five children, ranging in age from thirteen years down to fifteen months. The oldest, Edward, was disabled and, as the evening celebrations progressed, a message was received to say that he was unwell. Elizabeth Boyle went next door to check on him and was shortly followed by her husband.

They were expected to return to the wedding breakfast and, when they didn't, Archibald MacGregor went next door to check that Edward junior's indisposition was not serious. Entering the Boyle's house, he found Elizabeth sprawled on the kitchen floor dead. Thirteen-year-old Edward and his fifteen-month-old brother were in the room, the youngest boy fast asleep and his older brother incapable of speaking to explain what had happened. Elizabeth had a small bruise on the left-hand side of her face and her husband had an abrasion on his fist, as if he had punched someone.

The house was near to the police station and a constable arrived within minutes. Thirty-two-year-old Boyle told him 'It is all right, constable. I am the guilty party'.

Boyle was arrested and charged with his wife's murder. He appeared before Lord Anderson at the Glasgow High Court on 7th

September 1927, when the charge against him had been reduced to one of culpable homicide – of committing, but not intentionally, an act that ultimately resulted in a person's death.

Boyle's defence was that his wife had been very drunk and attacked him with a breadknife, so he had hit her twice in self-defence. She had fallen over, her head hitting a chair as she fell and, assuming that she was in a drunken stupor, he had left her lying on the floor and gone to bed.

Medical evidence suggested that Elizabeth had been hit or beaten, either with a fist or a blunt instrument, causing her death from a haemorrhage at the base of her skull. However, it was deemed possible that this had been caused by her head coming into contact with a chair in falling.

The Boyles' eight-year-old son, Charles, gave evidence in court, stating that his parents were arguing and he had seen his mother leaning over the kitchen table with a bread knife in her hand, although he had not actually seen her trying to attack his father. His father had hit his mother twice and, at that point, his father put him out of the room and he had seen no more.

Given that witnesses had earlier seen Elizabeth Boyle threatening her husband with both a breadknife and a smoothing iron and, in light of the medical evidence that she could have sustained her fatal injury by falling and hitting a chair, the jury found Edward Boyle not guilty and he was discharged from court.

Greenock, Renfrewshire

In June 1903, a wedding party dressed in their very best assembled in Greenock to celebrate a marriage. The only person who wasn't there was the bride and, after waiting for as long as they possibly could, the disappointed groom and the guests left the wedding venue.

Earlier that day, the groom had given his wife-to-be £40 to furnish their future home – the equivalent of almost £3500 today. Later that evening, she sent him a telegram, instructing him to return all the wedding presents to those who had given them, stating that she had decided that she preferred to go on her honeymoon by herself.

Limekilns, near Dunfermline

Coal trimmer Richard Colville and his fiancée Grace Adamson Ferguson, the daughter of the landlord of The Ship Tavern, Limekilns, were married on 14th June 1905. Reverend Robert Alexander of the United Free Church, Dunfermline, was reaching the end of the ceremony. The ring had been placed on Miss Ferguson's finger and she was about to sign the register when she suddenly fainted.

The wedding guests became ever more concerned as she failed to come round and a doctor was sent for. Dr Lee arrived but was only able to pronounce the thirty-eight-year-old bride deceased, citing the cause of her death as heart failure in all likelihood brought on by excitement.

Glasgow, Lanarkshire

On 6th October 1926, lamplighter John McMonigle took a cab to St Peter's Roman Catholic Church where he was to be married at 8.30 a.m. He was accompanied by his twin brother, Michael, who was to act as his best man.

On the way, the cab stopped at Kelvin Street to collect the bride from her home. John and his brother got out of the cab and walked up the steps to the front door. As they did, Michael, who was walking a little in front, heard John stumble and fall. He went back to help him and, to his horror, found that John was dead. Although a doctor was quickly sent for, it proved impossible to revive him.

Glasgow was in the grip of an influenza epidemic at the time and John had been suffering for the previous three weeks. He had been determined to get well for his wedding and had seemed almost fully recovered, if a little weak. A post-mortem examination found that he had died from acute cardiac dilation and heart failure, as a consequence of influenza.

Ayr, Ayrshire

Thirty-six-year-old Jane Dick had known cattle dealer Quintin Young since she was seventeen years old. In fact, she knew him very well indeed, as the couple produced seven children together. Yet in spite of their close relationship, forty-six-year-old Quintin had never lived with Jane but continued to live at home with his father. Although the couple spoke numerous times about getting married, there never seemed any hurry to do so.

In 1905, Quintin fell gravely ill with Bright's disease and began to consider marriage more seriously, wanting to legitimise the births of his five surviving children. He asked several relatives whether getting married to Jane would make their children legitimate and, having decided that it would, he asked his father to make arrangements for a vicar to visit his home on 1st June 1905. When the vicar arrived at the house, he asked Young if he knew why he was there. 'Yes, to make Jeannie (sic) my wife' replied Young.

The vicar went through the wedding ceremony, during which Young sweated profusely. When it came to signing his name in the register, Young was too weak to do so, so the vicar suggested that he made his mark with a cross. His father (also named Quintin) and his niece signed the certificate as witnesses to the marriage.

Less than five hours after his wedding, at just before midnight, Young died and, in the aftermath of his death, his father and his siblings took his new bride to court, claiming that he was not mentally capable of entering into the contract of marriage and therefore the marriage wasn't binding. Because no traditional banns had been read before the ceremony, there was an additional doubt about its legality.

The case was heard in the Court of Session before Lord Johnston, who first dealt with the fact that no banns had been read. This was a death-bed wedding and all parties concerned were aware of that, including the groom himself. Thus, although unconventional, the marriage was legal.

Young's family had brought a doctor into court. Dr Burns and the family all described the bridegroom as being 'in a torpid state' throughout the ceremony, arguing that he was not intellectually capable of giving matrimonial consent. Johnson found that, Young had accepted paternity of his children and had regularly contributed to their upkeep – indeed, two of them had actually lived with him at his father's home. There was no question that, in the days before the wedding, Young had made enquiries about whether or not getting married to the children's mother would make them legitimate and this seemed to be his main concern. Johnston decreed that Young was capable of giving his consent to the state of matrimony and the wedding was therefore legal and binding.

Wales

Cardiff

In 1924, Ellen Thomas and her family waited at Cardiff Registry Office for more than an hour for her bridegroom, coal trimmer George Guinea. Sadly, Guinea didn't show up, nor did he send any explanation for his absence, leaving his distressed and humiliated bride to return home still unmarried.

Two days later, Miss Thomas's father happened to bump into Guinea and asked him why he had jilted his daughter.

'I am very sorry. I was married abroad and have a wife in India.' Guinea explained.

Miss Thomas went on to sue Guinea at the Cardiff Sherriff's Court for breach of promise, fainting in distress as she gave her evidence. The court awarded her £150 in damages.

Near Cefn, Breconshire

David Harris of Penmoylan Farm went to give his cattle some hay on the morning of 10th May 1910. As he entered the barn where the animals were housed, he saw his farm labourer standing against a post near a wall. Knowing that twenty-four-year-old Thomas Davies was due to get married that morning, Harris called out 'Tom'. When there was no reply, he approached Davies, only then noticing that he had a cord wrapped tightly round his neck. Harris quickly cut the cord but Davies had hung himself and was beyond saving.

Coroner Mr W.R. Jones later held an inquest at which one of the chief witnesses was Davies's fiancée, Annie Knight of Merthyr. Annie stated that, the day before their wedding, they had gone to buy wedding rings and also a new suit for Davies to wear at the wedding. Annie was with her fiancé until around ten o'clock that evening. There was no quarrel between them, Davies was sober and she fully expected their wedding to go ahead as planned the next morning.

David Harries told the inquest that Davies had worked for him for about eighteen months and was a completely satisfactory employee. He had handed in his notice about a month earlier, announcing that he was going to be married. 'He was a most jolly fellow, always happy' stated Harris.

The rings and some brooches that Davies had purchased for his wedding were found in his pocket, along with 10½d in coins and a short note written in pencil, which read: *'My dear Kate you are the only one I love in this world and we will meet in the next, I hope. So I am going to the next world. Your loving Tom K.H. xxxx'*

Nobody knew who the mysterious 'Kate' in the letter was and, although the farmer had an eighteen-year-old daughter named Kate Harris, he wasn't aware of any relationship between her and his farm hand.

Addressing the jury, coroner Mr Jones told them that there was no trace of any insanity in Davies's family but that they, the jury, would have to be very careful about determining the condition of his mind. Throwing away a life was, in Jones's opinion, sufficient evidence that the mind was unhinged.

The jury returned a verdict of 'suicide while temporarily insane'.

Barry, Glamorganshire

Lance-Corporal John Peterson had been on active service in the East since 1914 and, in January 1919, he took his first leave in order to marry his fiancée, twenty-two-year-old Elizabeth Seaward from Barry.

Tragically, Peterson caught influenza, which developed into pneumonia and he died shortly before their wedding. Elizabeth herself fell ill with 'flu on what should have been their wedding day and died soon afterwards.

Aberavon, Glamorganshire

On 15th December 1893, twenty-year-old Annie Maria Davies was walking back to Ystalyfera, near Swansea, in preparation for her wedding the following day. It was a dark, stormy night and very windy and, when Anna was found drowned on the morning on which she should have married, it was assumed that she had been blown into the canal and been unable to extricate herself.

Penalt, Monmouthshire

On 24th April 1913, Miss Mary Ann England and Mr Frederick J. Honeywell were married at Penalt Church. As the bride and groom were being driven from the Church to the reception. They had barely progressed two hundred yards, when Honeywell suffered a seizure and became unconscious.

He was rushed to Monmouth Hospital, where he died later that night, his new wife by his side.

Blaenau Ffestiniog

A wedding was celebrated in Blaenau Ffestiniog on 7th July 1894, at which William Evans was asked to fire a canon in celebration.

As Evans was busy preparing the cannon, he absent-mindedly took his lighted pipe out of his mouth and slipped it into his pocket, quite forgetting that he had caps and cartridges in there. The resulting explosion blew off one of his legs and mutilated his body so badly that he died within minutes.

An inquest later recorded a verdict of 'accidental death'.

Rhydyfelin, Glamorgan

On 17th March 1909, Annie (or Hannah) Hopkins took her husband before magistrates accusing him of desertion.

Annie had married Edwin J. Hopkins on his twenty-first birthday on 31st December 1908. Yet the couple had never lived together and, after their wedding, Annie went to her home in Rhydyfelin, which was next door to 'Bridge Stores', the shop owned by Edwin's father.

Annie told magistrates that Edwin had refused to provide a home for her and the baby they were expecting. She claimed that he had 'got her into trouble' and had married her to avoid disgrace to his family.

Hopkins told the court that he had married Annie as a favour because she was in trouble. However, it was not his child and he insisted that he had never agreed to maintain her or to live with her. Annie and her family paid for the entire wedding – even her wedding ring. 'It didn't cost me a halfpenny' Edwin boasted.

'You did a good service for someone else then?' commented one of the magistrates sceptically.

In spite of the fact that the shop had a sign over the door which read 'Hopkins & Son', Edwin swore that it belonged solely to his father and the '&Son' had been painted by mistake, by a signwriter who had not fully understood his instructions. Edwin claimed that his father didn't pay him a wage but that he worked for his board and pocket money alone.

His father agreed with Edwin's assertion that his son had no claim on the shop, explaining that he had added the '& Son' to the sign to give Edwin some encouragement.

Magistrates ordered Edwin to pay six shillings a week maintenance and also to pay his wife's court costs.

Monmouth, Monmouthshire

On 9th June 1847, Richard Evans married Sarah Willis at the Independent Chapel in Monmouth. Mrs Willis was a widow, her previous husband, Phillip, having committed suicide in 1840, after first murdering their daughter, Ann.

Evans, who was in his seventies, was a widower. Knowing that she was dying, the first Mrs Evans had apparently urged him to marry again as quickly as possible '…so that he might have someone to wait upon him and take care of him.' Evans obliged his first wife by marrying within two months of her death – to her sister!

To further complicate the family relationships, one of Mrs Willis's daughters was married to one of Evan's sons.

Both Evans and his new bride dressed in mourning for their wedding.

Swansea, Glamorgan

On 13th October 1872, fourteen-year-old Bessie Green was waylaid as she walked to Sunday School and 'decoyed away' to London by a woman. Soon afterwards, they were joined by Henry Barnes, the father of one of her friends, who was a livery keeper at The Black Horse Inn on Rutland Street, Swansea.

On 16th October, Bessie and Barnes were married by special licence at St-Martin-in-the Fields. The wedding certificate clearly states that Bessie was a minor, while her bridegroom was reported in the contemporary newspapers to be '…on the dark side of fifty.'

The couple returned to Swansea by train and, as they were walking home from the station, Bessie's father and brother-in-law suddenly appeared out of the dark and snatched Bessie away, leaving Barnes angrily demanding the return of his wife.

Bessie was taken back to her father's house, to where Henry later sent a messenger with a copy of the marriage certificate. There seemed to be some dispute as to the bride's true age, with Mr Green claiming that she was only fourteen, and her new husband arguing that she was almost eighteen and could therefore marry whomever she pleased.

Records seem to show that the couple went on to have three children together – Gertrude, Florence Ethel and Henry Reginald, the last two named dying as infants. Henry himself died in 1879 and Bessie went on to remarry in September 1881, when she was twenty-three years old.

Magor, Monmouthshire

Twenty-two-year-old railway fireman George Barron from Newport was due to marry Sarah Clissold on Boxing Day 1898. He visited his fiancée at her home in Magor on Christmas Eve, when she asked him if he had got the money to pay for the wedding. George admitted that he hadn't, but promised that he was going to get it from his uncle the next day.

He saw Sarah at her sister's house on Christmas Day, when she was disappointed to realise that he was drunk. She asked him again if he had the money to pay for their wedding and George swore to her that he had a sovereign. Yet when Sarah demanded to see it, he could produce only eight shillings in cash.

Sarah was furious to realise that he had spent their wedding money on whisky and told him that she was not going to marry him. At this, George became very agitated and tried to grab her by the throat. Sarah pulled away from him and left the room and when her sister went in to ask George to leave, he told her that he would '...go and make it right with the water'.

Newport Bridge (author's collection)

He left the house at around five o'clock in the afternoon and was seen walking across Newport Bridge over the river Usk. A little later, he was seen to struggle in the water, eventually sinking opposite Spittle's Wharf. Boats were immediately launched but only his hat was retrieved from the river.

His body was not found for almost a month, when it was washed up at Magor Pill. On 23rd January 1899, Coroner Mr. M. Roberts-Jones held an inquest at The Wheatsheaf Inn, Magor.

Several witnesses testified that Barron had been '...a little strange' for two or three weeks before his intended nuptials, and that he was anxious that he wouldn't have enough money to pay for everything. Nobody thought him to be suicidal.

Sarah Clissold told the inquest that she and Barron had been courting for three years. About fifteen months earlier, she had broken up with him after a quarrel, at which he threatened to commit suicide and pretended to drink some turpentine and liniment. She claimed that Barron could be very excitable, particularly when he was in drink.

The inquest jury returned a verdict of 'found drowned', making no judgement on whether or not Barron had actually intended to commit suicide or whether his death was a simply an attempt to win back his fiancée that went badly wrong.

Pontypridd, Glamorgan

Miss Sarah Jane Davies met labourer William Lawrence Willey in London in 1919 and after courting for a while, they became engaged. On 21st December 1920, he travelled to her home in Clydach, ready for their wedding at Pontypridd Registry Office three days later.

On the morning of the wedding, Miss Davies left her purse containing her life savings of £2 12s in the living room. A while later, Miss Davies's father made a jocular remark about her standing him a drink and she told him that she couldn't, as she had left her purse at home. Willey had been the last person to leave the living room and, as she said this, she noticed his face going bright red.

When the wedding party reached Pontypridd, Willey made an excuse to leave for a few moments but never returned. After waiting for an hour, the disappointed bride returned home, to find her purse and all her money missing.

Willey was arrested at his home in Brixton by the Metropolitan Police and charged with stealing his intended wife's purse. Brought back to Wales to appear before magistrates at Porth, he claimed that he had never seen the purse or the money. He told the Bench that he had come down to Clydach on the understanding that there was a job for him and, on finding that there wasn't, he went back to London.

Magistrates found him guilty as charged and he was sentenced to four months' hard labour. They commented that it had been a particularly dishonest and cruel act to allow his fiancée and her parents to go to the expense of hiring a car to take them to the Registry Office, only to slope off when they got there.

Note: The contemporary newspapers give varying dates for the wedding. Most state that it was to occur on 24th December but some report that Willey came down from London on 28th November, with the wedding due to take place on 4th December.

Bargoed, Glamorgan

In June 1914, a car called to collect a wedding party at Bargoed to take them to the church in Hengoed. Bride Miss Annie Owen and her sister who was acting as her bridesmaid, bridegroom Edward Williams and best man, John Argust, were intending to collect the vicar on their journey but the car had only travelled a few hundred yards to the corner of Henry Street and Park Road, when it hit the kerb, collided with a brick wall and overturned.

Annie and her sister and Edward managed to scramble from the car, their clothes torn but, apart from a cut to Annie's hand, their injuries were not serious, mainly scrapes and bruises. The driver escaped unscathed, while the best man was less fortunate, ending up trapped underneath the car.

Numerous bystanders had been on the street to watch the bride and groom leaving the house, and people hurried to lift the car off Argust. Fortunately, his injuries amounted to nothing more serious than some scrapes on his face and a badly bruised shoulder. The car however was a write off and a cab had to be summoned to convey the party to church, where the wedding went ahead as planned. The car diver later explained that he had been temporarily blinded by the rice that was thrown at the couple getting in his eyes.

Swansea, Glamorgan

In October 1914, Katie Bater and John 'Jack' Henry Marley married at Swansea Registry Office. However, the bridegroom wasn't actually Marley but twenty-year-old Ernest Charles William Haines, who had been offered a sovereign by Katie to stand in for her fiancé, a gunner in the Royal Field Artillery, who was then in hospital in France. The newlyweds enjoyed a wedding reception then went their separate ways.

When Katie didn't pay Ernest the money she had promised him, his sister Dorothy went to the police and the 'happy couple' were both arrested. Both were charged with making a false declaration to the registrar of marriages at Swansea, with the object of a marriage ceremony. Kate was additionally charged with obtaining £8 2s 6d soldiers' marriage allowance on false pretences from Morriston Post Office.

Before magistrates, Dorothy Haines stated that she had heard Katie and her brother having a conversation, after which Katie told her 'Ernie has promised to marry me in Jack's name. I will give him a sovereign.'

Katie's mother had attended the wedding and was suspicious that something was not quite right. Sophia Bater challenged Ernie that he was not Marley but Ernie assured her that he was.

'You look nothing like him' commented Sophia, to which Ernie replied 'I've been ill'.

The case was sent to the Glamorgan Assizes, where the couple appeared before the Right Honourable Lord Coleridge. Ernest Haines told the court that he had only accepted Katie's offer because he needed money to feed his two little brothers. Katie meanwhile explained 'I done it because I was in trouble. I wanted Marley's name for the baby, that is all. I am sorry.'

The judge took a dim view of the case, telling the defendants that it was necessary in the public interest that such frauds on the public purse should be dealt with most severely. Turning to Katie, he told her 'You were mean enough not to pay Haines the money you promised him. There seems to have been little honour among thieves in this case. I look upon you as the author of Haines's downfall, for without your persuasion of him, he could not have effected this fraud.'

Coleridge took into account Haines's previous good character in sentencing him to two months' imprisonment. Katie was less fortunate, receiving a sentence of eight months' imprisonment with hard labour, which she served in Swansea Prison.

Amazingly, on her release, it appears as if she and Haines actually got together and tried to make a go of their relationship as in December 1921, Katie charged Haines with desertion. He was also summonsed for allowing his wife and child to become chargeable to the Swansea Union.

Before magistrates at Swansea Police Court, Katie explained that she had lived with Haines for three years until 1918, when they parted after a quarrel after he received a letter from a girl from Durham. Katie moved out of the marital home and went back to live with her mother. She asked Haines for a divorce, claiming that he couldn't provide a home for her.

Katie denied allegations that a Danish man named Neilson was the father of her youngest child, although she admitted to having relations with another man, which she claimed was only so that Haines had the necessary grounds to divorce her, which he still refused to do.

Magistrates dismissed the case for desertion and the case against Haines of leaving his wife chargeable to the Union was withdrawn.

Note: Many contemporary newspaper reports give Katie's name as Kate or Katie Baker. Records suggest that Bater is the correct surname.

Bibliography

Aberdeen Press and Journal

Armagh Standard

Barnsley Independent

Belfast Morning News

Belfast Weekly News

Boston Guardian

Boston Gazette

Coventry Evening Telegraph

Daily Mirror

Derby Daily Telegraph

Devon and Exeter Gazette

Dundee Courier

Exeter and Plymouth Gazette

Freeman's Journal

Hull Daily Mail

Illustrated Police News

Lancashire Evening Post

Larne Times

Leeds Mercury

Leicester Chronicle

Liverpool Echo

Mansfield Reporter

Musselburgh News

Newcastle Journal

Northampton Mercury

North Eastern Daily Gazette

Nottinghamshire Guardian

Reading Mercury

Sheffield Independent

Skegness Standard

South Notts Echo

Taunton Courier

The Guardian

The Scotsman

Western Daily Press

Western Mail

Western Morning News

West Sussex Gazette

Worcestershire Chronicle